BLACK ✦ STARS

AFRICAN AMERICAN MILLIONAIRES

✦

OTHA RICHARD SULLIVAN, ED.D.

JIM HASKINS, GENERAL EDITOR

John Wiley & Sons, Inc.

Copyright © 2005 by Otha Richard Sullivan. All rights reserved

Published by John Wiley & Sons, Inc., Hoboken, New Jersey
Published simultaneously in Canada

Design and composition by Navta Associates, Inc.

For general information about our other products and services, please contact our Customer Care Department within the United States at (800) 762-2974, outside the United States at (317) 572-3993 or fax (317) 572-4002.

Wiley also publishes its books in a variety of electronic formats. Some content that appears in print may not be available in electronic books. For more information about Wiley products, visit our web site at www.wiley.com.

Library of Congress Cataloging-in-Publication Data:
Sullivan, Otha Richard, 1941–
    African American millionaires / Otha Richard Sullivan ; Jim Haskins, general editor.
        p. cm. — (Black stars)
    Includes bibliographical references and index.
    ISBN 0-471-46928-9 (cloth)
1. Wealth—United States 2. Millionaires—United States. 3. African Americans. I. Haskins, James, 1941– II. Title. III. Black stars (New York, N.Y.)
    HC110.W4S86 2004
    305.5'234'092396073—dc22
                                                                        2004014694

Printed in the United States of America
10 9 8 7 6 5 4 3 2 1

CONTENTS

FOREWORD

For too long African Americans have been portrayed in many quarters as the poorest of society, who, in the past and even now, rely on government subsidies. Certainly they are not overly perceived as a real part of the monied gentry. However, many of us know that this is a well-worn stereotype, which persists in spite of steady, visible, and documented economic gains by many African Americans today. Even among the most casual observers, it is clear that African Americans are integral participants who contribute much to the economy. Many are well ensconced in the ranks of the middle class. Others have found themselves comfortably embedded among the wealthiest in the nation. It is the latter group that Otha Sullivan writes about. He gives us a glimpse into the lives of some African Americans who rose to take their place among an elite group of African Americans who became millionaires, and some of them billionaires. Through their profiles, readers are taken through a fascinating journey among people who defied all odds, without exception, to reach the economic pinnacle.

The stories of these African Americans enlighten us by revealing a little-known facet of American history. These profiles are not just about rich millionaires. They are much richer in content. They are about people who came from humble beginnings and through hard work, strategic business investments, and maybe even a little bit of luck, achieved astonishing economic success. These women and men have stories that are inspiring.

The first African American millionaire was William Alexander Leidesdorff, a successful pioneer businessman in the Bay Area. He is credited with starting the first public school in San Francisco. His story is merely the beginning.

Other nineteenth-century African American millionaires were women, such as Mary Ellen Pleasant, an astute businesswoman with sharp political acumen. Nearly a century before Rosa Parks, the mother of the modern civil rights movement, refused to relinquish her seat on a city bus in Montgomery, Alabama, Pleasant filed a suit against a San Francisco company for refusing her a ride on a city trolley car because of her race.

These are only two of many African American millionaires profiled by Dr. Sullivan, from the time when slavery reigned right up to the present day. They hailed from all over the nation, and they were successful in spite of their circumstances, race, or time and place in history. None of these millionaires were born with a silver spoon in their mouths. From all indications they did make their fortunes the "old-fashioned" way: they earned it.

This collection of unique life stories is as American as apple pie. It is of the pick-yourself-up-by-your-bootstraps-and-soar genre. It is purely in the tradition of Horatio Alger; only the faces have changed. Some of these African American millionaires are well known; others are unknown. Through these profiles, Otha Sullivan debunks several myths about African American wealth. One is that the recent celebrity wealth among sports figures and entertainers represents the only path to economic success and riches open to African Americans. That is not so. Another is that the rank of millionaires from Reconstruction to the early twentieth century was an exclusive preserve of whites. That is also not so.

Dr. Sullivan's book is an important contribution that fills in some gaps in African American history. It not only educates, it entertains and inspires. Susan Anderson, writing on black wealth, stated, "African American entrepreneurs have a unique story to share [about economic] . . . success. But the real success lies in a near universal commitment to community and civic service." She was right and Dr. Sullivan backs her up.

This commitment to others in the black community (and beyond) is a common strand that can be found throughout the profiles. In reading about these millionaires and their pursuit of riches, Otha Sullivan makes sure that we know about their considerable philanthropic works. These African American millionaires could be a model for all the wealthy, regardless of race, color, or ethnicity.

Winston Churchill once stated, "We make a difference by what we get. We make a life by what we give."

These African American millionaires made a life.

Betty W. Nyangoni, Ph.D.
Education Consultant
Washington, D.C.

ACKNOWLEDGMENTS

A special thanks to Stedman Mays, my literary agent at Clausen, Mays and Tahan, for his support in the development of this project and efforts in finding a home for this book.

Thanks to Carole Hall, my editor at John Wiley & Sons, who believed in this project and made numerous helpful suggestions. Camille Acker also contributed to the editing and photo research, keeping me on task. Jim Haskins accepted this work in the Black Stars biography series. I am grateful to each of these remarkable individuals for their support.

Special thanks to Kate Bradford, editor at Wiley, and Devra K. Nelson, senior production editor.

Thanks to Dr. Betty Nyangoni for providing support and assistance as developmental editor. I shall always be grateful to her for helping me with my first professional journal article. Many thanks to Dr. Georgia Williams for the many hours spent with me in developing this and other projects.

A special thanks is given to Chuck Patrick of Jackson State University, who also provided assistance in the development of this book. His invaluable input helped me to complete this project.

Many thanks to Gretchen Buckles at Alcorn State University for her support of this project.

INTRODUCTION

✦

African Americans have used hard work, determination, and persistence to overcome incredible odds. After three hundred years of slavery, the Emancipation Proclamation finally freed U.S. slaves in 1865. By just five years later, in 1870, the year of the first census to enumerate blacks by name, many African Americans had made great strides. The U.S. Census for that year shows that blacks had already gained wealth, which was often in the form of property. My own great-great grandfather Levin Booth, a property owner in Covington County, Mississippi, was wealthy when compared to whites in the same census area. His success was repeated many times throughout the country.

Some African Americans became so successful that they became millionaires. But for many, it wasn't enough to achieve only wealth. These millionaires did their best to pass on their good fortune. African Americans have a tradition of supporting organizations and movements whose purpose is to uplift the race. These millionaires had achieved self-sufficiency and wanted to help others do the same. They often shared their wealth with those who were less fortunate.

This is called philanthropy, meaning love of humanity. Among African Americans, philanthropy has its roots in black churches and mutual aid associations. The associations were started in the late 1700s to provide assistance to people in the black community. Early African Americans were also large contributors to the Underground Railroad and the Abolitionist Movement. The Underground Railroad was a system of homes and buildings where runaway slaves could hide on their way to freedom in the North. The Abolitionist Movement was organized by people who supported the abolition of slavery.

The earliest examples of African American philanthropy are found in the Fraternal Order of Prince Hall Masons, founded in 1775; Boston's Sons of Africa Society, founded in 1788; and the African Union Society, founded in 1781. These organizations assisted black families by providing housing, financial assistance, and support for the poor.

William Alexander Leidesdorff, born in 1810 in the Virgin Islands, is considered to be the first African American millionaire in this country. His philanthropy extended to public schools and the less fortunate.

At about the same time, Mary Ellen Pleasant, often called the Mother of Civil Rights, gained wealth and influence in San Francisco. Pleasant used her business abilities to create a fortune some say was worth $30 million in her day. She fought for the equality of African Americans and supported the fight for the abolition of slavery. Her advocacy led to African Americans gaining the right to testify at trials in California, as well as the right to ride on San Francisco streetcars.

The tradition of sharing the wealth continued into the latter half of the nineteenth century. Biddy Mason, an enterprising former slave, settled in Los Angeles, became a successful businesswoman, and made her fortune in real estate. She gave to the poor, regardless of race, and founded the First African American Methodist Church in Los Angeles.

Black millionaires and philanthropists have also made significant gifts to institutions serving African Americans. In 1989, Oprah Winfrey gave generously to Morehouse College with a $1 million donation. This gift was followed in 1997 with a donation of another $1 million. Businessman and former National Basketball Association (NBA) star Michael Jordan contributed $1 million to the University of North Carolina at Chapel Hill to establish an institute for families at the university's school of social work. Lawyer Willie Gary pledged $10 million in 1992 to Shaw University, an historically African American college in Raleigh, North Carolina.

Mat Dawson, a forklift driver at Ford Motor Company from Monroe, Louisiana, has donated more than $1 million to various colleges and churches. These institutions include the United Negro College Fund, Wayne State University in Detroit, the National Association for the Advancement of Colored People (NAACP), and Louisiana State University, Shreveport. Dawson's contributions have given students an opportunity to do something he did not: complete an education.

Crispus Attucks Wright, the son of a former slave in Louisiana, gave $2 million to his alma mater, the University of Southern California (USC) Law Center, to establish scholarships in his name. A prominent attorney, he used his legal skills to fight real estate covenants, which prevented African Americans from having equal housing opportunities. He was inspired to give because of a $50 scholarship he received when he was a law student at USC.

These African American millionaires gained wealth in a variety of ways, but they all did the same thing: they gave back. Whether donations of money or donations of time, these individuals made it their goal to help others.

PART ONE

✦

THE
EARLY YEARS

WILLIAM ALEXANDER
LEIDESDORFF

(1810–1848)

The first African American millionaire was William Alexander Leidesdorff, a founding father of California, who arrived in San Francisco in the Spanish territory called "California" as early as 1839. He became a Mexican citizen and settled in Yerba Buena, which became San Francisco, in 1841. An enterprising businessman, Leidesdorff built the first hotel in San Francisco, named the City Hotel. Leidesdorff also was active in educational and civic activities and was responsible for establishing the city's first public school.

William Alexander Leidesdorff was born in the Virgin Islands to William Leidesdorff, a Danish sugar planter, and Anna Marie Spark, a native woman of African ancestry. They had five children. Young William was fascinated with boats. People who knew him well weren't surprised when he left the Virgin Islands as a young man and made his way to New Orleans to engage in maritime trade. The port of New Orleans was a busy one and was ranked fourth in the world in terms of size and traffic.

✦ **Maritime** means shipping and navigating on the sea.

Leidesdorff became a master at sailing. He traveled between New Orleans and New York, carrying cotton and buying and selling other merchandise. With the money he made, he purchased a 106-ton schooner, the *Julia Ann*, and quickly established a lucrative business of his own. Around 1838, Leidesdorff started making trips to Hawaii, transporting Hawaiian sugar to the mission at Yerba Buena. Then he returned to Hawaii with hides and tallow.

In 1841, Leidesdorff settled in Yerba Buena. San Francisco Bay had a reputation for being the best harbor on the Pacific Coast. At that time, California was not a state (it joined the Union as the thirty-first state in 1850). William saw limitless possibilities in California. African Americans at the time were prohibited by law from owning land, but with Mexican citizenship, he obtained a grant to purchase forty-one lots, or thirty-five thousand acres, in the town of Yerba Buena, which later became part of the city of San Francisco. He also built the largest and most impressive home in the city on land where the present-day Bank of America Tower stands in San Francisco. In addition to the property in San Francisco, William was awarded a Mexican land grant to establish Rancho Rios de los Americanos in what is now eastern Sacramento County.

Leidesdorff started an import-export business that specialized in tallow, otter skins, and hides. He also built a large shipping warehouse and lumberyard. Soon after settling in California, Leidesdorff also became active in politics, serving as vice consul to Mexico. During his leadership, Leidesdorff lent support to the Bear Flag revolt. It occurred on June 14, 1846. A band of some thirty American settlers, disgruntled with Mexican control of the California territory, seized Colonel Mariano Guadalupe Vallejo and told him that he was a prisoner of war. The American settlers hoisted a flag emblazoned with a drawing of a bear, a lone star, and the words, "California Republic," and declared independence, no longer wanting to be a part of Mexico. Four years later, the United States claimed California as a state.

His success in politics never deterred him from his first love:

sailing. Leidesdorff launched the first steamboat to sail on San Francisco Bay. The boat, named the *Sitka,* had been purchased from a Russian fur company in Sitka, Alaska. In November 1847, the steamboat made its way to Sacramento. The voyage took six days and seven hours. Unfortunately, the next day a storm wrecked the ship, and it was unable to sail again.

AFRICAN AMERICANS HELP SETTLE CALIFORNIA

Besides William Leidesdorff, many other African Americans helped to settle California.

James Pierson Beckwourth, a hunter and a fur trader, discovered what became known as the "Beckwourth Pass" over the Serra Nevada Mountains. Beckwourth fought in the California Revolution in 1846. Beckwourth Pass, located a few miles northwest of present-day Reno, Nevada, was traversed by thousands of pioneers and gold seekers to California. The Western Pacific Railway would later use Beckwourth Pass as a gateway to the west. Many African Americans came to Northern California as a result of the development of the Western Pacific Railroad.

Maria Rita Valdez, an African American woman, was the ranchero, or landowner, of Rancho Rodeo de Aguas, now known as Beverly Hills.

Don Pio Pico, whose grandmother was an African American, was the last Mexican governor of California. Born at the Mission San Gabriel Los Angeles in 1801, he became governor twice, once in 1832 and then again in 1845 to 1846. Pico also built an elegant hotel and the first three-story building in California.

African Americans were also a part of the founding of the Pueblo of Los Angeles in 1781. Of the forty-four *pobladores,* or settlers, twenty-six were either full-blooded or part African. They were from farming communities in Sinalos and Sonora, which were provinces of New Spain, now known as Mexico.

Leidesdorff was a founding father of California for many reasons, including building San Francisco's first shipping warehouse and first hotel, and organizing the area's first professional horse race.

Leidesdorff died of brain fever at the age of thirty-eight in 1848. City leaders held a large funeral and gave tribute to this distinguished citizen, hanging flags at half-mast from all military barracks and ships in the port of San Francisco. Guns were fired as the funeral procession moved through the winding streets to Mission Dolores, where Leidesdorff's body was laid to rest beneath the stone floor.

At the time of Leidesdorff's death, the California Gold Rush was just beginning. Although Leidesdorff's estate was deeply in debt, the discovery of gold on his property changed that. The property was soon worth more than a million dollars and would have made Leidesdorff the wealthiest man in the state.

✦ In 1848, California businessmen James Marshall and John Sutter discovered gold. They tried to keep their discovery a secret, fearing all of the people who would now want to come to California. The secret soon got out, though, and people came from all over the country to strike it rich in what became known as the **Gold Rush.** The journey to California was very hard, however, and of those who made it all the way, most did not find their fortune.

✦

PART TWO

THE
CIVIL WAR YEARS
AND
RECONSTRUCTION

MARY ELLEN
PLEASANT

(1814–1904)

Mary Ellen Pleasant was a pioneer in the fight for the rights of African Americans. In the mid-nineteenth century, she helped fugitive slaves and made numerous trips to rescue them. Pleasant later became one of the most prominent and wealthy people in San Francisco, with a fortune worth more than $30 million in her day. She contributed money to the Underground Railroad and other abolitionist causes.

Pleasant was born a slave near Augusta, Georgia. She said she was the daughter of John H. Pleasant, a Virginia governor's son, and an enslaved Haitian woman. At age nine, a white planter purchased her out of slavery and sent her to New Orleans where she became a servant for Louis Alexander Williams,

> ✦ The **Underground Railroad** was a network of over three thousand homes and other "stations" that helped escaping slaves travel from the southern slave-holding states to the northern states and to Canada.

a merchant in Cincinnati. Little Mary was promised her freedom after serving Williams, but he broke his promise. Williams, a businessman heavily in debt, made Mary a bonded servant. "Bonded" servants

could be white or black and were forced to work for a number of years to pay back a debt. But Williams was jealous of his wife's affection for Mary and placed her in informal indenture. Mary was forced to work for nine more years for an old Quaker merchant, Grandma Hussey, in Nantucket, Massachusetts.

Pleasant was a mulatto, a person who had both black and white ancestry. She looked like she was white and was told never to reveal her race. In Nantucket, she took the name Mary Ellen Williams. She was still young,

✦ **Quakers** are members of a religious group founded in the 1600s. They were strongly anti-slavery and often leaders in the Abolitionist Movement.

but she worked hard in Grandma Hussey's general store and could remember the account of any customer. Pleasant was quite intelligent and gifted in reading and writing.

While in the service of Grandma Hussey, Pleasant adopted the Quakers' belief in abolition and the principles of equality. Many blacks joined with white abolitionists in the early 1800s to fight against the horrible institution of slavery. Their work made it impossible to ignore the issue. Abolitionists formed various anti-slavery societies that petitioned Congress, made anti-slavery speeches, and served as "conductors" on the Underground Railroad.

TEACHING SLAVES TO READ

At the time, the teaching of reading to slaves was forbidden in slave states. Punishment for such a "crime" could lead to imprisonment, beatings, or death. Slave owners knew that if slaves knew how to read, they would be more difficult to control. They understood the power of reading and realized that individuals who read can liberate themselves.

In 1841, Mary Pleasant's period of service with her Quaker guardian ended. She moved to Boston and became a paid tailor's assistant and church soloist. She found more than work in Boston; she also found a husband, James W. Smith, a successful contractor and merchant and the owner of a plantation in Virginia. Mary and James both worked for the abolitionist movement. James risked his life to spy for William Lloyd Garrison, an abolitionist and publisher of *The Liberator*.

Just three years after they married, James died, but Pleasant continued her work with the abolitionist movement. She used a $45,000 inheritance from her husband for abolitionist causes. New Bedford, Massachusetts, was her home, but Pleasant began traveling to the South and bringing slaves back to freedom. She used many disguises to enter plantations and helped hundreds of slaves escape. She would meet slaves along the way and tell them about escaping. Plantation owners hated Pleasant for what she was doing and tried to stop her, even offering rewards for her capture.

By 1851, life was dangerous for Mary Pleasant. With slavers on her trail, she moved to New Orleans. She had remarried and went to live with the family of her new husband, John James Pleasance. She remained in New Orleans for a few months, but Louisiana planters were determined to capture her. Her husband left Mary in New Orleans and traveled to San Francisco to find a safe haven for his wife. Hearing rumors of an impending capture in New Orleans, Pleasant sailed around the tip of South America from New Orleans to San Francisco to join her husband, a trip that took four months.

On that trip, Pleasant met Thomas Bell, a young Scottish merchant, who would become her business partner and close friend. Their association would lead to wealth in the millions for both. After arriving in San Francisco on April 7, 1852, Pleasant changed her name to Mrs. Ellen Smith. Her fair skin allowed her to pass for white. The Fugitive Slave Act allowed escaped slaves and even blacks who had always been free to be taken into slavery.

Despite the dangers, San Francisco in the 1850's had many opportunities for African Americans. There were job opportunities as cooks, bakers, waiters, barbers, tailors, teachers, and shoemakers. There were even African Americans who ran boarding houses. With the advent of the Gold Rush, buying, renting, and selling property became a quick source of wealth for these people.

Pleasant once told the *San Francisco Examiner* that she came to San Francisco with $15,000 in gold coins, her husband's family's money, which she lent to several businessmen. She probably handled more money during pioneer days in California than any other black person.

Pleasant became the proprietor of a number of boarding houses for wealthy businessmen. She also established successful restaurants that catered to the rich. Within a short time, Pleasant became a business advisor to wealthy businessmen, which provided her with insight into gaining more personal wealth. In the black community, Pleasant was highly regarded for her efforts to assist them. She was often referred to as the "Black City Hall."

Pleasant was the most talked-about woman in San Francisco. In a time when African Americans were rarely mentioned in the press, more than one hundred articles were written about her achievements as a philanthropist, abolitionist, and freedom fighter.

Armed with her tremendous wealth and social influence, Pleasant began a campaign to help ex-slaves fight for equality. She helped organize the Colored Conventions that petitioned the California legislature to provide individuals of color the same rights afforded to whites. She lobbied for the rights of blacks to testify in court, to ride on the city's streetcars, and to have access to jobs, which were starting to be given to European immigrants. Her fight for civil rights led to her filing a suit against two trolley lines whose conductors refused her passage. To ease the economic plight of blacks, Pleasant employed many blacks in her businesses and taught them how to start their own.

A decision by the U.S. Supreme Court on March 6, 1857, stirred

Pleasant to continue her fight for the freedom of all: that decision concerned the Dred Scott case. The Court decided that an African American could not be a citizen of the United States and therefore did not have the rights of a citizen. (Citizenship for African Americans would come nine years later when the U.S. Congress approved the fourteenth amendment to the Constitution.)

Pleasant was determined to do something about this reversal in the struggle for freedom. She returned east to help John Brown, a Kansas abolitionist. Pleasant bought land in Canada to provide homes for slaves that Brown had freed. Two years earlier, in 1856, Brown had killed five pro-slavery men at Pottawotamie Creek in Kansas. This action was the beginning of what was known as "Bleeding Kansas," a time of many conflicts between pro- and anti-slavery groups. Pleasant gave John Brown $30,000 to help his cause. The money would be used for his raid on the federal arsenal in Harper's Ferry, Virginia. Brown wanted to gather weapons from the arsenal and use them to free slaves. Pleasant traveled to Harper's Ferry to tell slaves of the impending raid.

MIFFLIN GIBBS AND PETER LESTER

Pleasant was not alone in her fight for equal rights. Mifflin Gibbs and Peter Lester were two wealthy African American businessmen in California. With only a dime in his pocket, Gibbs moved to California in 1850. He and Lester opened a store called Lester and Gibbs Boots and Shoes. They were actively involved in the anti-slavery movement and joined the Colored Conventions in California, of which Pleasant was a member. Gibbs was also one of the publishers of *Mirror of the Times*, a San Francisco paper for African Americans.

On October 16, 1859, John Brown's raid began. Brown was unsuccessful, and he was hanged for treason on December 2, 1859. Mary Pleasant barely escaped being hung for treason as well for her part in supporting the raid.

The Civil War and the Emancipation Proclamation finally freed slaves, but Pleasant's fight was not yet over. She started several court battles to test new civil rights legislation. Pleasant won $500 in damages in 1868 after suing the streetcar company that refused to allow her board a train because she was black. The case of Pleasant vs. the North Beach and Mission Railroad Company granted blacks the right to ride on public transportation. The case went all the way to the California Supreme Court and set a precedent for civil rights for blacks in California.

Pleasant also found herself fighting against the California Legislature, which approved one bill after another restricting the access of any African American to the judicial system. Although California officially had no slaves, the state continued to pass laws that supported slavery and slaveholders. Conditions were so bad for many African Americans that some considered settlement outside the United States.

After the Civil War, Pleasant stopped passing as a white woman. She let everyone know she was African American. Pleasant continued to run her businesses and help those who were less fortunate, finding jobs for African Americans wherever she could.

In 1904, Mary Pleasant died in San Francisco. She was buried in Tulocay Cemetery in Napa, California. Her tombstone reads, "Mother of Civil Rights and Friend of John Brown." She had lost much of her wealth, but at the time of her death, she left an estate of more than $300,000 to those who had helped her in her old age.

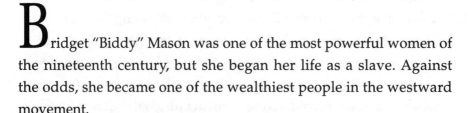

BRIDGET "BIDDY" MASON

(1818–1891)

◆

Bridget "Biddy" Mason was one of the most powerful women of the nineteenth century, but she began her life as a slave. Against the odds, she became one of the wealthiest people in the westward movement.

She was born on August 15, 1818, on the Mississippi plantation owned by Robert Marion Smith and Rebecca Smith. When she was eighteen, Robert Smith gave Biddy Mason as a personal servant to his wife as a wedding gift. Mason soon became the mother of three daughters, Ellen, Harriet, and Ann. Robert Smith was their most likely father.

Around 1847, Smith decided to become a Mormon and moved his family and slaves to the Utah Territory. Brigham Young, the leader of the Mormon Church, had recently established a community there. The journey to Utah was more than two thousand miles by horse and buggy. Mason walked behind the wagon train for the seven months it took to reach Salt Lake City. In addition to taking care of her own children, she was responsible for many chores on the trail, such as herding the cattle, cooking, and serving as a midwife to women and

livestock. Smith, his family, and slaves remained in Utah for four years.

In 1851, they joined a 150-wagon caravan and moved to San Bernardino, California, another Mormon community. Mason and her three daughters walked across the hot desert that lay between Utah and California. Along the trail, she met Charles and Elizabeth Flake Rowan. Unlike Mason and her daughters, the Rowans were free blacks. They encouraged her to sue for freedom because California was a free state, not a slave state like Mississippi.

When Mason arrived in California, she met Charles Owens, a successful African American businessman who would become Mason's son-in-law. Owens helped her petition the Los Angeles district court for her freedom. When Smith and other whites sympathetic to slavery heard the news of Mason's petition for freedom, they attempted to capture the former slaves and forcibly take them to Texas. The judge issued a protective order for Mason and her children and for the other former slaves owned by Smith. They were placed in jail for their protection while awaiting the court's ruling.

Since testimony by blacks in a court of law in California was not allowed, Smith tried to persuade the court that Mason and her children wanted to go with him to Texas. Mason had no way to deny this. However, the judge wanted to hear Mason's side, so he talked to her and her children in his chambers. They told the judge the truth: that they wanted to stay in California and be free. After three days of hearings, Mason won freedom for herself and her daughters.

Deciding that Los Angeles was a good place for the family to settle, she found employment as a nurse and midwife for a Dr. John Griffin. As she was paid only $2.50 a day, Mason had to be frugal with the money she earned. Her goal was to become self-sufficient and purchase some land and a home for her children. Accustomed to hard work and determined to provide a good life for her daughters, she soon became financially independent.

Although California was a free state, Mason and other African Americans did not enjoy the same civil rights given to whites. In addition to not being allowed to testify in court, African Americans could not receive a public education, settle on public lands, or vote. Mason did not let any of those restrictions stop her from achieving her goals.

In 1866, she became one of the first African American women to own land in Los Angeles. After saving for ten years, she paid $250 for two lots on Spring Street, which is now the center of the commercial district of Los Angeles. Mason lived at 331 Spring Street from 1866 to 1891. She told her children to keep the land in the family; owning property was a way to maintain their freedom and independence.

Mason soon realized that the land was quite valuable. She sold a portion of it in 1884 for $1,500. A commercial building with rental spaces was constructed on the remainder of the property. Mason's fortune soared to more than $300,000 by 1890, the equivalent of about $2.4 million today.

Biddy Mason gave to many charities in the Los Angeles area because she felt blessed and wanted to share her good fortune with others. She made it her mission to provide food and shelter for the poor. Every day, a line of men and women formed at 331 Spring Street to get a hot meal. Her home became a home to others and was named the House of the Open Hand.

In 1872, Mason and her son-in-law Charles Owens founded and financed the Los Angeles branch of the First African Methodist Episcopal Church. It was the first African American church in Los Angeles, and the first church services were held in the living room of Mason's home.

During 1861 and 1862, what became known as the Great Flood and the drought that followed devastated many people in California. Mason reached out to those in need and made her account at a local grocery store available to flood victims. Many lovingly called her "Auntie Mason" or "Grandma Mason."

EARLY AFRICAN AMERICAN CHURCHES

The first African Baptist Church of Savannah, Georgia, is the oldest African American Church in North America. It was established in 1773. The first African Methodist Episcopal Church was founded in 1787 in Philadelphia. Richard Allen led the withdrawal of African American Methodists from the white Philadelphia congregation where they had worshipped. Allen was the founder and first pastor of Mother Bethel African Methodist Episcopal Church in Philadelphia.

Biddy Mason died on January 15, 1891. Her life was filled with supporting and caring for others, but she was buried in an unmarked grave at Evergreen Cemetery in the Boyle Heights area of Los Angeles. Almost a hundred years passed before a tombstone was unveiled that acknowledged her contributions. More than three thousand members of the First African Methodist Episcopal Church, as well as Tom Bradley, the first African American mayor of Los Angeles, attended the ceremony.

Today, visitors to Los Angeles can go to Biddy Mason Park at the Broadway Spring Center, built on property Mason once owned. This land is now some of the most valuable real estate in the city of Los Angeles.

ANTHONY
OVERTON

(1864–1946)

A pioneer in black cosmetics and skincare products, Anthony Overton was born a slave in 1864 in Monroe, Louisiana. After the Civil War, young Anthony and his family left the South, like other African Americans of their time, hoping to find a better life farther north. They moved to Kansas, where he attended public schools. There Anthony had a chance that his parents never did—to go to school and learn to read and write.

Overton worked hard and went on to receive a degree in law from Washburn Law School in Topeka, Kansas. Soon after being admitted to the Kansas Bar, he was appointed to the municipal court bench in Topeka. Despite his success, he was not happy with his career in law and decided to start a business.

In 1898, Overton moved from Topeka to Kansas City, Missouri. In a short time he founded the Overton Hygienic Products Company. With less than $2,000 to start his business, Overton first tried making baking powder. But when he realized that women's cosmetics and hair products were more lucrative businesses, Overton began to create

cosmetics especially for the complexions of African American women.

In 1911, at the age of forty-seven, Overton moved his business operations to Chicago. Within nine months, his company grew into a multimillion-dollar business employing more than four hundred people. The Overton Hygienic Products Company became one of the nation's top producers of African American cosmetics. By 1912, the company manufactured fifty-two products and it continued to grow, shipping products as far as Egypt, Liberia, and Japan.

Overton had successfully met one need in the community, and yet he wanted to meet another—to start a magazine for African Americans. In 1916, Overton published the first edition of *The Half Century*, a reference to the fifty years that had passed since the Emancipation Proclamation. The magazine covered the arts, politics, and business. It also included a legal advice column, fiction by African American writers, and positive news about the community. The magazine had a successful nine-year run and ended publication in 1925, but by then Anthony Overton had already moved on to new ideas. In 1926, he started a newspaper, the *Chicago Bee*, which became popular on Chicago's South Side. The *Chicago Bee* even coined a nickname for a Chicago neighborhood—"Bronzeville"—which was the area near the South Side where African Americans lived.

Overton met another community need when he established the Douglass National Bank and founded the Victory Life Insurance Company the following year. Douglass National, the first African American–owned national bank, was successful until the stock market crash of 1929 and the Great Depression that followed. Most of the banks in Chicago and around the country, including Douglass National, were forced to close.

✦ The **Great Depression** was a period of financial difficulty in the United States. Millions of people were unemployed, and even those who weren't faced poverty. The stock market crash in 1929—when people and businesses alike lost much of their money—helped to start the Great Depression.

Overton worked hard during his lifetime and received recognition for his many accomplishments, including the Harmon Award and the NAACP Spingarn Medal. He died in 1946.

ABRAHAM LINCOLN
LEWIS

(1865–1947)

Abraham Lincoln Lewis was the first African American millionaire from Florida. He was a leader who possessed many talents, but like many African American children of his time, he never went to school.

Abraham was born in Madison, Florida, the same year the Emancipation Proclamation was signed. His parents, Robert Lewis and Julia Brown, named their new son after Abraham Lincoln, the president and emancipator of the slaves. His birth was a special occasion because he was the first person in his family born free. After his birth, the Lewis family moved to Jacksonville in search of a better life. It took time for them to find work and establish themselves. They refused to give up, however, and soon they received much-needed help from the African Methodist Episcopal Church.

Abraham's father worked as a blacksmith, but his parents wanted better for their son; they wanted him to get an education. Young Abraham wanted to enroll in public school, but times were hard for his family. His parents had to give up their dream for their son, because they needed him to work and help earn money. Abraham began working

at the Dexter Hunter Lumber Mill as a water boy. He earned very little and worried that he would always be poor. He decided that he would start saving a small portion of his earnings, so that one day he wouldn't have to worry about money.

Life began to change for Abraham when his employer recognized his intelligence and initiative. He was promoted to the position of foreman, a kind of supervisor, who was the highest-paid black man at the mill. He worked there for more than twenty years. During that time, Lewis took some of his savings and invested in a shoe store, the first to be owned and operated by blacks in Jacksonville. By saving carefully and investing prudently, he was well on his way to becoming an entrepreneur by age twenty-three. Around this time, he also married Mafry Sammis, the great-granddaughter of a wealthy planter, writer, landowner, and political activist.

Lewis was not just a businessman. He also was involved in organizations, such as the Masons, that helped to empower African Americans. The Masonic Temple was the focal point for the African American community's commercial and fraternal activities. At the time, Masonic organizations provided insurance for African Americans, since insurance companies owned by whites would not cover them. While serving as treasurer for the Masons, Lewis developed special skills in managing money and learned the insurance business as well.

In 1901, Lewis helped to establish an insurance company for African Americans. With only $100 and faith on the part of Lewis and the six other founders of the company, the Afro-American Life Insurance Association was chartered by the State of Florida. Lewis served as treasurer.

The Afro-American Life Insurance Association provided low-cost policies to its customers for health and burial insurance. By the end of the first year, the company began to turn a profit of just over $50 a week, but the founders soon faced an obstacle when almost the entire downtown area of Jacksonville, more than one hundred and forty blocks, burned down. The fire left nearly ten thousand people homeless and at least seven people dead. Eartha White, the clerk for the company, risked her life to save its supplies and important insurance records. She knew that the records were invaluable and that the survival of the company depended on them. After the fire, the company was moved to Lewis's home. His twenty-two-room mansion, Sugar Hill, in the affluent Springfield Heights neighborhood, was one of the few houses that managed to avoid destruction. The company was able to rebuild quickly.

Lewis became the president of Afro-American in 1919. Over the years, the company had prospered, and its headquarters were moved to a new building. Revenue increased with the purchase of the Miami Mutual Insurance Company. Thanks to Lewis's hard work and a clear vision, the company continued to grow. It also acquired the Chathorn Mutual Life Insurance Company, thereby expanding its business operations into Georgia.

As a successful entrepreneur, Lewis founded the Negro Business League and the National Negro Insurance Association. Lewis continued to have a strong faith in God and gave back to the community that helped him become successful. By his example he inspired many African Americans, young and old, to enter business.

Jacksonville's commercial district, called "the bricks," was characterized by thriving businesses that included theaters, churches, newspapers, and the Masonic Hall. In 1935, Lewis established the all-black Lincoln Golf and Country Club where African American celebrities from around the country came to play or dine. Boxer Joe Louis was a frequent visitor.

That same year, Lewis bought a large stretch of seashore: two hundred acres in Nassau County known as American Beach. Lewis wanted it to be a place where families didn't have to worry about discrimination, and he wanted his employees to have someplace to vacation. In the beginning, individuals could buy oceanfront lots for $200. Now those same lots range from $85,000 to over $100,000.

American Beach was the only place on the north Florida coast where blacks were allowed. During the early part of the twentieth century, African Americans were forbidden from using such public facilities as beaches. As a result, they began establishing their own beach properties across the country, like American Beach, as well as Idlewilde in Michigan.

In 1936, Abraham Lincoln Lewis was recognized for his accomplishments in business and philanthropy. Wilberforce University in Ohio awarded him an honorary Doctor of Laws and Letters degree.

ALONZO FRANKLIN HERNDON: FROM SLAVE TO ENTREPRENEUR

Alonzo Franklin Herndon was born a slave in 1858 near the town of Social Circle ,in Walton County, Georgia. Everyone around him was a sharecropper, but Herndon did not want to work in the red-clay fields of Georgia.

With only one year of formal education, he learned to cut hair in Jonesboro, Georgia, and opened his first barbershop there in 1878. In 1882, he moved to Atlanta, and there he became one of the city's top barbers on fashionable Peachtree Street.

Herndon invested his income in real estate and became the largest African American owner of property in Atlanta. In 1905, he was approached by two prominent black ministers, one of whom was Reverend Peter Bryant, pastor of the Wheat Street Baptist church. Reverend Bryant had formed the Atlanta Benevolent and Protective Association. Herndon bought the association for $140, forming the Atlanta Mutual Insurance Company, which later became the Atlanta Life Insurance Company. It would later become the largest African American–owned insurance company in the United States. Herndon died in 1927 at the age of sixty-nine. At the time of his death, he was worth millions.

Lewis made generous contributions to various organizations throughout his life. He gave money to all of Florida's black colleges, and served as trustee and treasurer of Edward Waters College. Created after the Civil War, it is the oldest college for African Americans in Florida. Lewis's generosity financed the education of many young men and women.

In 1947, Lewis died, owning more property than any other black person in the state of Florida and an estate worth more than $1.5 million. On May 3, 2001, the city of Jacksonville unveiled a historic marker for the Afro-American Life Insurance Company at the corner of Ocean and Union Streets.

PART THREE

◆

INTO THE NEW CENTURY

MADAME C. J. WALKER

(1867–1918)

Madame C. J. Walker grew up in poverty, unable to read or write, surviving one hardship after another. She was born in Louisiana in 1867, one year before Congress passed the fourteenth amendment granting African Americans full citizenship. Her parents were Minerva and Owen Breedlove, former slaves, and they named their daughter Sarah. From sunrise to sunset, even as a child, Sarah worked alongside her parents in the cotton fields near the shores of the Mississippi River. Her parents died before she turned six, leaving her older sister Louvinia to care for her.

Sarah wanted to escape her hard life, so at age fourteen she married Moses McWilliams. She often said she married at the age of fourteen in order to get a home of her own. She was a widow by the time she was twenty. How her husband died is unknown, but now Sarah had a child, Lelia, to care for on her own. Despite the difficult circumstances, she called Lelia her "wealth." From 1887 to 1905, Sarah and her daughter moved twice, to Vicksburg, Mississippi, and then to St. Louis, Missouri. Sarah supported them by working as a washerwoman for white families.

While still a young woman, Sarah had faced enough catastrophes for a lifetime. Then her hair began to fall out, and she began experimenting with various mineral and animal oils to find a remedy.

Sarah would later say that a man had appeared to her in a dream and told her how to cure her problem. Although some ingredients were from as far away as Africa, Sarah followed the instructions from her dream and made the remedy. In a few weeks, her hair had grown back. Sarah believed her mixture could have miraculous results for other women as well.

In 1905, feeling revived, Sarah moved to Denver, Colorado, to help her sister. There she started selling her secret hair-care formula to her new neighbors, and she met and married C. J. Walker. She liked being called Madame C. J. Walker, and she used that name for the rest of her life, although she left her husband three years later. Leaving Mr. Walker behind, Madame Walker and Lelia moved to Pittsburgh, where she founded the Lelia College of Beauty to teach the Walker system. In 1910, Madame Walker moved her offices to Indianapolis. A plant was constructed that became the headquarters for the Walker enterprise, which was called the Walker College of Hair Culture and Walker Manufacturing Company. The company provided employment for some three thousand people, whom Madame Walker called "hair culturists," "scalp specialists," and "beauty culturists." They dressed uniformly in spotless, starched white shirts and long black skirts.

Business thrived. The Walker system even found its way to Europe. Josephine Baker, the singing and dancing sensation of Paris, had her hair styled using the Walker method. She became a walking advertisement for Madame Walker.

While Lelia helped sell the products through the mail, her mother toured the country, encouraging other women to buy Walker products and to be as independent as she was. She surrounded herself with loyal, capable workers and became one of the nation's largest employers of African American women. Her employees often went to their clients' homes to style their hair. Walker encouraged them to be inventors, too. Several women emulated her and became highly successful in the hair-care business. Madame Walker was guided by the business acumen of Annie Turnbo Malone (see next chapter).

Having worked hard all her life, Madame Walker at last began to enjoy her success as a millionaire. She was the first American woman, black or white, to earn a million dollars. Vertner Tandy, an African American architect, built a twenty-room mansion for her called Villa Lewaro at Irvington-on-the-Hudson, New York. The building cost $250,000, a large sum in 1917, and the mansion cost $500,000 to furnish.

Walker gave generously to the NAACP, the Tuskegee Institute, and various charities that supported black orphans. She also gave generously to the Daytona Normal and Industrial Institute for Negro Girls, founded by her friend, Mary McLeod Bethune. Madame Walker also provided scholarships for students at Palmer Memorial Institute, a private high school for blacks in Sedalia, North Carolina, founded by another friend, Charlotte Hawkins Brown.

Madame Walker was always busy and took little rest, even when her doctors told her she should because of her high blood pressure. In 1919, at a time when her empire was at its height, she became very ill while in St. Louis. She returned to her home in New York and died there on May 25. In her will, she left the business to her daughter, as well as $100,000 to build a school for girls in West Africa. She also made sure that the Madame C. J. Walker Manufacturing Company would always have a woman president.

Lelia Walker died suddenly in 1931, leaving the remaining estate to the NAACP. However, because the organization could not afford the upkeep of Villa Lewaro, the property is now privately owned. Today, the Madame C. J. Walker Manufacturing Company is a museum in Indianapolis. The museum sponsors theater and musical performances and operates a cultural arts education program for youth.

ANNIE TURNBO
MALONE

(1869–1957)

Annie Minerva Turnbo Malone invented hair and skin products even before Madame C. J. Walker did. Like Madame Walker, Malone became a millionaire by successfully marketing her products. At one time, she was worth $14 million.

Born to Robert and Isabella Cook Turnbo on August 9, 1869, in the small town of Metropolis, Illinois, Annie was the tenth of eleven children. While the other children were playing games, Annie entertained herself by braiding strings attached to a Coca-Cola bottle. She had fun pretending that she was braiding real hair.

Annie attended Peoria, Illinois High School, where she discovered that she had an interest in physical science. Her favorite subject was chemistry, but she never outgrew her fascination with hair care. She often braided other girls' hair after school. Her friends used goose fat, soap, and heavy oils to straighten their hair. Annie noticed that these mixtures often caused the girls to lose their hair and develop scalp problems. She believed there must be a way to straighten hair without damaging it. If there was a way, she was confident that she could find it.

In 1900, when Turnbo was thirty-one, she left Peoria, and moved to Lovejoy, Illinois. There Turnbo set up a laboratory to develop hair-care products.

She worked countless hours experimenting with ingredients that did not harm the hair and scalp. Then her interest expanded beyond products just for hair. Her mission became clear—to give African American women their own beauty products—and she did.

In 1900, Turnbo patented the first pressing comb to straighten hair. In 1902, she moved to St. Louis, Missouri, seeking new opportunities. There she set up shop and hired sales people. She trained her agents by going door-to-door with them, selling her products and giving free beauty treatments to demonstrate their quality. Madame Walker was one of Turnbo's earliest sales agents, joining her around 1903.

Annie Turnbo continued to build up her business. Its phenomenal growth was attributed to her shrewdness, persistence, hard work, and commitment. In 1917, she purchased an entire city block and built a multimillion-dollar complex, which included a vocational school called Poro College. This successful enterprise was located near Sumner High School, which opened in 1875 as the first African American school west of the Mississippi.

By 1926 Malone had a vast empire for her products. She had developed and manufactured a series of hair products, deodorants, skin creams, pressing oils, and other toiletries. These products were sold in all major U.S. cities, as well as in Europe, South America, and many African countries. By the age of forty-eight Turnbo had become the major stakeholder in the black cosmetics and beauty industry.

To name her product line, Turnbo chose a West African word, *Poro*, meaning "physical and spiritual growth." Black newspapers advertised her hair straightening-and-conditioning products, but she always said the best advertisement was a satisfied customer. Her agents had a twenty-four-hour turnaround time for shipping products to customers.

BLAZING A TRAIL

In addition to its function as a vocational school, Poro College also became a cultural institution for African Americans in St. Louis. It had a theater, an auditorium, and a cafeteria. Entertainers including Roland Hayes and Bessie Smith offered concerts at Poro's plush concert hall. In a short time, Poro College was franchised in more than fifty cities. More than fifty thousand African American cosmetologists were trained at Poro, including Madame C. J. Walker, who later made a fortune of her own.

Poro College trained African American beauticians, barbers, and salespeople. It became the first institution to teach cosmetology for the black consumer. The college had classrooms for teaching beauty culture, a barbershop for cutting African American men's hair, and well-equipped laboratories for developing new hair and skin products.

After settling in the Ville district of St. Louis, Malone began to share her wealth. In 1919, she donated $10,000 for the construction of a new building for the St. Louis Colored Orphans' Home, which had been founded in 1881.

Malone believed in giving back to the community. At one time, she was reported to have supported two full-time students in every black land-grant college in the United States. She also donated $25,000 to Howard University during the 1920's.

Along the way, Annie married Aaron Malone. He was the chief manager and president of Poro until 1927. In a much contested divorce, Annie negotiated a settlement of $200,000 with her husband. Aaron Malone claimed that the success of the Poro business was due to his business skills and ability to market the company.

By 1920, Annie Turnbo Malone was worth more than $14 million. Six years later, she had more than seventy-five thousand agents selling her products door-to-door throughout the United States, the

Caribbean, and other countries. In the late 1920s, Poro, like so many other businesses, went under during the Great Depression.

In 1932, Malone courageously decided to start over in Chicago. She purchased a manufacturing plant in Chicago's white manufacturing district and set up shop on a street that became known as Poro Block. Malone faced hard times between 1943 and 1951, with several lawsuits filed against her to claim excise taxes. Her failure to pay real estate taxes led to the sale of most of the Poro property. By 1950, the government had control of the Poro empire. Annie Turnbo Malone died in Chicago's Provident Hospital on May 10, 1957, of a stroke. She was eighty-seven years old. At the time of her death, her fortune had been depleted to $100,000. As a testament to her life's work, thirty-two Poro College branches still were in operation in the United States at that time.

ROBERT SENGSTACKE
ABBOTT

(1870–1940)

Robert S. Abbott, the founder of the *Chicago Defender* newspaper, began his road to wealth with an investment of just twenty-five cents. The first issue of the *Chicago Defender* came out on May 5, 1905. Abbott printed three hundred copies in the kitchen of his landlord's apartment in Chicago. For five years, he was the only employee of the paper, serving as editor, ad salesman, and circulation director. By 1920, Abbott was printing over two hundred thousand copies weekly.

◆ From 1915 to 1925, more than 1.5 million southern blacks migrated to the North in search of better jobs, housing, schools, and health facilities. This became known as the **Great Migration.** Some have estimated that at least 110,000 African Americans migrated to Chicago between 1916 and 1918, which tripled the city's black population.

Abbott, like other successful African Americans, did not permit discrimination or prejudice to define the heights to which he could aspire. Abbott's newspaper was published in Chicago, but it was read across the country by millions of African Americans. It became so important to them that Abbott's call for blacks to come to the North to find jobs and less discrimination helped

to encourage the Great Migration from the South to northern cities in the 1900s.

Robert S. Abbott, the son of former slaves, was born in 1870 in Frederica, St. Simons Island, Georgia, to Thomas and Flora Butler Abbott. Thomas Abbott died of tuberculosis when Robert was one year old. Robert and his mother moved back to Savannah, where his mother met and soon married John Sengstacke. Robert was taught the value of hard work at an early age and began working as an errand boy at a grocery store. His mother required him to pay ten of the fifteen cents a week he earned for room and board.

Abbott became interested in printing at an early age when he worked as an apprentice to a printer at a newspaper.

✦ An **apprentice** is someone who agrees to work for a certain period of time to learn a trade or skill.

He also learned the newspaper trade from his stepfather, who published a local paper. Abbott long dreamed of owning his own newspaper. He admired Frederick Douglass, the abolitionist and speaker, who founded the newspaper the *North Star*. Robert knew the power and influence that Douglass's paper had on African Americans. He wanted to develop a new newspaper that would be a powerful weapon against discrimination and prejudice.

In the fall of 1886, young Robert entered Beach Institute, an American Missionary School in Savannah, to prepare for college. He faced considerable prejudice from lighter-skinned African Americans because he was dark skinned. Unhappy at the school, he set his sights on learning a trade at Hampton Institute, in Virginia. This school was founded on April 1, 1868 to train freed slaves. After finishing Hampton in 1896 with a degree in practical training as a printer, he returned to the Savannah suburb of Woodville and began working part time as a printer and a schoolteacher.

Realizing the importance of knowing the law, in particular the protection it offered to African Americans, Abbott pursued a law degree in 1897 at Kent College of Law in Chicago. He received his degree in

1899, the only African American in his class. After law school, he faced the kind of discrimination he hoped to challenge in courts when he was denied the right to practice law due to racial prejudice, but he tried to open law offices in Gary, Indiana, and Topeka, Kansas, anyway. Abbott did not succeed and decided to return to Chicago.

In 1905, Abbott returned to his first love and began publishing the *Chicago Defender*. The paper was not successful at first, and Abbott considered closing it down. His landlord, a Mr. Lee, stepped in and permitted him to use the kitchen in his apartment as the newspaper's office. When Abbott became sick with pneumonia, Lee helped him get better, even accepting partial payments for his rent and food.

With the financial and moral support Lee offered, the *Defender* began to prosper. Within five years, he was able to hire a full-time employee, J. Hockley Smiley. In a short time, the circulation of the *Defender* surpassed the three rival African American papers in Chicago. Positive news about African Americans and articles about discrimination and prejudice were absent from white papers, but not from the *Defender*. Abbott took on racial injustice, including the horrors of lynchings, and other issues that concerned his readers.

In 1918, with some of the money he had made from the newspaper, Abbott showed his appreciation for Lee's support and bought him and his family an eight-room house. Lee's daughter became an employee of the *Defender* and her son became a stockholder in the Robert S. Abbott Publishing Company.

Southern whites attempted to ban the distribution of the paper, believing it would encourage blacks to stand up for their rights. White distributors in the South refused to circulate the *Defender*. Some white groups, such as the Ku Klux Klan, attempted to confiscate the paper and threatened its readers. Even the federal government tried to stop it. But the *Defender* could not be stopped. Abbott used African American porters on trains to distribute the newspaper. African American entertainers also distributed the paper across the Mason-Dixon line.

THE MASON-DIXON LINE

The Mason-Dixon line is generally associated with the division between the Northern and Southern states (free and slave, respectively) during the 1800s and the American Civil War era. The line was drawn in the mid-1700s, more than a hundred years before the Civil War. This line was a settlement of a property dispute between Pennsylvania and Maryland. The surveyors of this 244-mile line were Charles Mason and Jeremiah Dixon.

The Missouri Compromise of 1820 established a boundary between the slave states of the South and the free states of the North. As part of this compromise, Missouri was admitted as a slave state, Maine as a free state, and territories in the Louisiana Purchase were defined as both free and slave.

The Mason-Dixon line was the boundary between the states of Pennsylvania and Maryland that extended west along the Ohio River to its mouth at the Mississippi River.

Because his newspaper originated in the North, Abbott was able to write stories that southern African American publishers feared would bring trouble to their businesses and employees. Abbott attacked the system of sharecropping that had replaced slavery.

In addition, Abbott provided first-hand coverage of the Red Summer Riots of 1919, a series of race riots in cities across the country. The *Chicago Defender* also provided one of the few forums for African American writers and poets. Its columnists included Walter White, president of the NAACP, poet Langston Hughes, and social critic W. E. B. DuBois. The early poems of Pulitzer Prize–winning poet Gwen-

✦ In the early 1900s, few African Americans owned land in the South. Black **sharecroppers** entered into agreements with white landowners to grow crops and in return receive only a small portion of the harvest. The landowners kept the rest. For a fee, the landowners provided seed, fertilizers, and provisions for African Americans to live on until the crop was harvested. To get these supplies, they borrowed against their earnings. Since their earnings were rarely enough to pay for these supplies, sharecroppers were often in debt after the harvest.

dolyn Brooks were published in the *Chicago Defender*. Abbott was also responsible for encouraging and providing financial support for Bessie Coleman, the famous African American pilot, to go to France for pilot training when she was refused acceptance to American flight schools.

The success of the *Chicago Defender* made Abbott one of the first African American self-made millionaires in this country and he was well recognized for his achievements, receiving honorary degrees from Morris Brown College and Wilberforce Academy. Abbott was also a member of the Hampton Institute's board of trustees. Abbott died on February 29, 1940. He bequeathed his paper to his heir and nephew, John Henry Sengstacke. Sengstacke assumed editorial control of the paper and continued his uncle's fight for full equality of African Americans. He founded the *Daily Defender* in 1956, one of three African American dailies in the country. Sengstacke died on May 28, 1997, after an extended illness.

On November 4, 2002, the Cook County, Illinois, Probate Court, which had overseen the company since the death of John Sengstacke, approved the sale of the *Chicago Defender*. It was purchased for $10.9 million by Real Times, Inc., a group led by Tom Picou, a former *Defender* editor and John Sengstacke's nephew.

Abbott was a leader in his advocacy for civil rights. He did not "bite his tongue" and informed whites as well as blacks about the plight of African Americans. Abbott confronted issues of racism head-on and did not fear any repercussions. He denounced racial inequities and informed his readers of the horrors of lynchings, assaults, and other atrocities against black Americans.

Abbott was regarded by many as the voice of black America. He appealed to southern blacks to leave bondage and move north for better opportunities in jobs, education, and housing. For more than thirty years, Abbott told the truth and made millions. His voice was welcomed by millions of African Americans and others who did not find the truth in white-owned newspapers about unjust conditions blacks faced in this country.

GASTON

(1892–1996)

Many African Americans of wealth had humble beginnings. Hard work, faith, and tenacity ensured their success. Arthur George Gaston's start was no different. He grew up poor in the small town of Demopolis, Alabama. The grandson of slaves, Gaston became one of the most powerful and wealthy men in the state of Alabama, as well as the nation. Gaston's investment interests and businesses were guided by the belief that they should empower African Americans. To this end, he established an insurance company, a bank, a motel, two radio stations, a construction business, and a realty and investment corporation. Gaston would eventually be worth between $30 million and $40 million.

Arthur Gaston was born on July 4, 1892, to Tom Gaston, a railroad worker, and Rosa Gaston, a cook. Arthur's father passed away when he was a little boy, and after his death, his mother moved to Birmingham in search of better job opportunities and housing. The city of Birmingham was established in 1871 where two rail lines crossed in the mountains of north-central Alabama. It was known for its huge

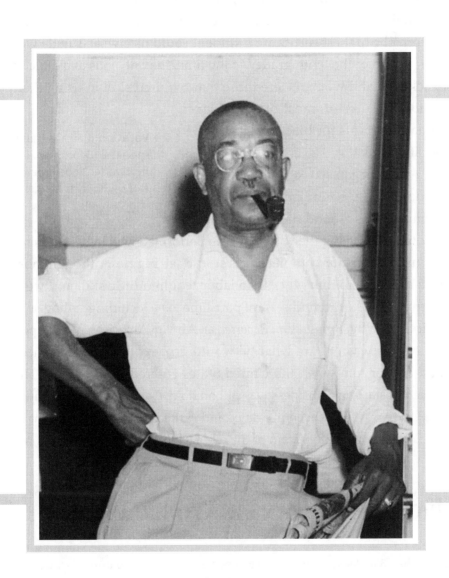

deposits of iron ore, limestone, and coal. The area's steel industry flourished and became one of Birmingham's leading employers.

Upon settling in Birmingham, Arthur enrolled in Tuggle Institute, a school where students received both a moral and an industrial education. The highest certificate a student could receive at Tuggle was completion of the tenth grade. At the time, the only jobs available to black men and women were those that required skill in using their hands. As a result, most of the educational programs for blacks taught only vocational skills.

> ♦ **Vocational** means training in a special skill for a job in a certain field, often jobs where people work with their hands.

Arthur began staying on the campus of the institute and earned money by performing tasks around the school. By all accounts, he was a gifted student who performed well in his studies.

In 1910, Arthur completed his studies at Tuggle. Although most jobs available to him other than labor required little skill and were often boring, he did find several part-time jobs, including selling subscriptions to the *Birmingham Reporter,* an African American newspaper.

Arthur wasn't sure what he would do next, but circumstances decided for him when the United States entered World War I. His dream of starting a business was put on hold. Gaston was drafted into the U.S. Army. He served in France and earned the rank of sergeant in the 317th Ammunition Train of the all-black Ninety-second Division.

AFRICAN AMERICANS IN WORLD WAR I

More than 350,000 African Americans served in segregated units during World War I. While most black troops were eager to fight, they primarily provided support services. Some units fought alongside French soldiers fighting against the Germans. France awarded them its highest honor, the French Legion of Honor, for their service.

After serving with honor in the military, Arthur Gaston returned to Birmingham. There he found that the social, economic, and physical condition of African Americans had not changed since he left for military service. While African Americans fought bravely in the war, discrimination and inequalities still faced them back at home. Rights that whites had, such as voting, adequate housing, equal employment opportunities, and health care, were denied African Americans.

Gaston was still hopeful that he would find a job with good pay with an employer who recognized his qualifications. He finally accepted a job at the Tennessee Coal and Iron (TCI) plant in Westfield, Alabama. Gaston was paid just $3.10 a day for a job building railroad cars. To make more money, he started a small business right in the plant selling his mother's homemade sandwiches and desserts to his coworkers. Gaston's business sense extended even further. He started lending small sums of money to the other workers with interest.

By 1920, African Americans had established fraternal, masonic, and other organizations whose primary objective was to empower other African Americans. Many of the groups started investment clubs, since banks did not lend money to blacks. Birmingham was one of the cities that used fraternal organizations to support businesses and encourage people to be economically independent. Gaston joined various business groups and was mentored by successful black businessmen such as Thomas Walker, Thomas C. Windham, and Oscar Adams. In the early 1920s Gaston married Creola Smith, who died during the first years of their marriage. There were no children from this union.

✦ **Interest** is a charge for a loan made by a person or business. It is usually a percentage of the amount of the loan.

Gaston stopped working at TCI around 1923 and went into business with his father-in-law, Abraham Lincoln "Dad" Smith. Gaston and Smith started a business called the Booker T. Washington Burial Society, which later became the Smith and Gaston Funeral Home.

Some years later, the business was incorporated and became the Booker T. Washington Burial Insurance Company in Fairfield, Alabama.

In 1939, Gaston married his second wife, Minnie Lee Gardner. They had one son who died.

Gaston's personal mission to empower African Americans socially and economically motivated him and his wife to establish the Booker T. Washington Business College. The school taught clerical skills to African American students. Graduates were then hired to work in Gaston's businesses, where Gaston mentored them and insisted that they save their earnings.

In 1954, Gaston's business vision led to the construction of the Gaston Motel, a place for African Americans to stay when they were denied rooms in white hotels. During the Civil Rights Movement in Birmingham, activists often stayed in the Gaston Motel.

Throughout the demonstrations, arrests, and deaths in Birmingham during this time, Gaston offered moral and financial support to movement leaders. When Dr. Martin Luther King Jr. was arrested and wrote his influential "Letter from a Birmingham Jail," it was Gaston who put up King's bail. Gaston believed his place in the movement was as a negotiator instead of as a demonstrator. When demonstrators were arrested, he often paid their bail. Using his influence as a businessman, Gaston met with white leaders and employers to negotiate equal rights for African Americans. His home and hotel were bombed, but Gaston continued to support the efforts of civil rights leaders.

African Americans were discriminated against and refused loans and mortgages at the white banks in Birmingham. Although blacks could open a savings account or a small account to save for Christmas, they could not get a loan. In 1957, Gaston founded the Citizens Federal Savings and Loan Association, which later became the Citizens Federal Savings Bank, a source for blacks to borrow money to build or purchase homes. By 1961 its assets exceeded $5 million.

Gaston also saw a need for activities for young people in the com-

AFRICAN AMERICAN BANKS

The first African American banks opened their doors for business in 1888. Two of the African American banks founded during that year were the Savings Bank of the Grand Fountain United Order of the Reformer, in Richmond, Virginia, and the Capital Savings Bank of Washington, D.C.

munity. He believed that sports, educational support, and positive role models could stop some young people from choosing the wrong path. In 1966, he founded and endowed the A. G. Gaston Boys Club, now known as the A. G. Gaston Boys and Girls Club. He donated $50,000 to the club as well as the proceeds from his autobiography, *Green Power*. His generosity in supporting youth programs continued throughout his life.

While many African American banks across the country faced difficulties and closed, Gaston's bank survived. More than half of the forty-three black-owned banks went out of business in the 1980s. Gaston's bank became the largest black bank in Alabama and the eighth largest in the country.

By 1987, at the age of ninety-five, Gaston made a decision to sell his insurance company and eight other corporations. Believing in his employees, he sold his holdings to them. The price of the stock was $3.5 million, even though at the time of the sale, the company had more than $34 million in assets and $726 million worth of insurance. Gaston continued to maintain control of the Citizens Federal Savings Bank and the Smith and Gaston Funeral Home.

Although Arthur George Gaston never finished high school, he received numerous honorary degrees. His awards as a distinguished businessman include *Black Enterprise* magazine's Entrepreneur of the Century, the Liberty Bell Award from the Birmingham Bar Association, induction into the Alabama Men's Hall of Fame, and Outstanding Service from the Boys Club of America.

On the eve of his one hundredth birthday, in January 1992, Gaston suffered a stroke. This illness did not keep him from reporting to his office for work four weeks later. This drive and determination helped him to overcome illness and old age.

Arthur Gaston passed away in 1996 at the age of 104. His longevity must have come from his stamina, good eating habits, tenacity, and a determination to keep physically fit and mentally alert throughout his life.

S. B.
FULLER

(1905–1988)

S. B. Fuller was a sixth-grade dropout, but he founded one of the most successful businesses of his time. His rise to wealth and influence began with a goal, a plan, and a desire. His talent for sales that began as a small child, selling products door-to-door, translated into a multimillion-dollar company.

Fuller was born in 1905 in the rural town of Ouachita Parish, Louisiana, to parents who were sharecroppers. The oldest of eight children, Fuller had to do the work of a grown man. His mother always reminded him that poverty was a choice. She did not want him to use hard times as an excuse to fail and remain poor. At age nine, he got his first job, driving mules. Working and going to school was difficult, but that problem was soon solved, because at the time, public school education for African Americans ended after the sixth grade. Young S. B. took on even more responsibility when his father left the family.

On her own, Fuller's mother packed up her children and moved to Memphis. S. B. was fifteen years old at the time. In two years his mother had died, and S. B. and his siblings were struggling to get by

on government assistance. He was devoted to his brothers and sisters and helped bring them up after the death of their mother.

Fuller was unhappy with the lack of job opportunities in Memphis and dreamed of moving North for a better chance. This dream he realized at age twenty-three, when S. B. hitchhiked to Chicago with less than a dollar in his pocket and a lot of faith that he would survive and do great things. This confidence was to become an asset in his future business ventures.

In 1934, S. B's life changed when he read a story in the local paper that listed the wealthiest men in Chicago. He noted that the president of Chicago Metropolitan Life Insurance Company made $50,000, but the president of Lever Brothers, a soap manufacturer, made more than $450,000. So he used his entire savings of $25 to join the National Laboratories, another soap manufacturer, as a distributor. Buying soap wholesale and selling it door-to-door on Chicago's South Side, Fuller worked hard so that one day he would have his own company.

By 1947, Fuller had saved enough money to purchase Boyer International Laboratories, a white cosmetics manufacturer. His ownership remained a secret so that white customers would not boycott the company because he was a black man. He continued to save money and was successful in starting another business, the Fuller Products Company, developing more than thirty products that salespeople sold door-to-door.

Lonesome for home, Fuller returned to his birthplace in Louisiana and continued his business there. He recruited salesmen to distribute his products, selecting mostly African American men in Louisiana and throughout the South. Whites resented his success and tried to bully him into closing his business and leaving Louisiana. Undaunted, Fuller and his distributors stayed and prospered. Many of the salesmen became wealthy from selling his products.

Fuller later returned to the Chicago area and built a $250,000 mansion in Robbins, Illinois. By 1960, Fuller had developed more than three hundred products, employed more than five thousand salespeople, black as well as white, and opened eighty-five branches of his company in thirty-eight states.

Fuller was a firm believer that African Americans could do anything that whites were successful in doing. He motivated his employees by offering rewards to his top salespeople, including cars for the top three in sales and bonuses to twenty-four other employees. His business continued to grow until sales exceeded $10 million. Fuller products, which included face creams, perfumes, lotions, and a full line of household needs, had great appeal to blacks and whites alike. In fact, more than 60 percent of his customers were white.

As he got older, Fuller turned his business acumen to newspapers, real estate, farming, and cattle. He purchased interests in two African American newspapers: The *New York Age* and The *Pittsburgh Courier*. He was one of the wealthiest African Americans of his time.

Fuller's success dimmed in the 1960's. The secret that had been kept for so many years about his purchase of a white company was revealed. The White Citizens Council, a southern organization of white men opposed to integration and equal rights for African Americans, found out that Fuller was the owner of the former Boyer Company and organized a boycott. At the time, African Americans were boycotting white businesses in the south in their quest for equal rights. To protest Fuller's ownership of Boyer and those African Americans boycotting white businesses, drugstores throughout the South removed the Boyer line of products from their shelves.

The boycott of Fuller Products nearly destroyed the company. To recoup his losses, Fuller turned his attention to other business opportunities. He purchased the South Center Department Store on Chicago's South Side, which became the Fuller Department Store.

Fuller would not permit adversity to affect his desire to be successful and sell quality products. In the 1970's, after several years of business problems, he attempted to revive his business. He was successful. His profits exceeded $300,000 in 1972.

Fuller, like other African American millionaires, was a mentor to others. Two of his employees, called "Fullerites," were Joe Louis Dudley, the owner of Dudley Products, and George Johnson, owner of Johnson Products. Both men became successful businessmen and millionaires.

Fuller always supported other African American businesses. He did not permit competition to get in the way of doing the right thing. When a fire destroyed the Johnson Products building, Fuller offered his facility to his former employee, and Johnson accepted. Some years later, Johnson would show his gratitude to Fuller when Fuller's business failed. In 1976, Johnson gave him two thousand shares of Johnson Products' stock worth more than $50,000.

John H. Johnson, a publisher, also offered goodwill and support in 1976 on the occasion of Fuller's seventieth birthday. At a testimonial dinner, Johnson presented Fuller with a check for $70,000, a gesture to help Fuller at a time he needed financial support to rebuild his business.

By 1976, Fuller was in failing health, unable to effectively guide the corporation he founded. Fuller wanted to find a capable individual to run his business. He immediately thought of Joe Dudley, who had worked for him. Fuller contacted Dudley in North Carolina and made him an offer to move to Chicago and become president of the Fuller Products Corporation. Remembering the guidance Fuller gave him as a young man, Dudley gladly accepted the offer and moved to Chicago. He managed the Fuller Company and his own business with excellence.

Fuller spent his lifetime uplifting and supporting African Americans. He served as head of the South Side chapter of the NAACP. Fuller was the first African American member of the National Association of Manufacturers. He served as the president of the Chicago Negro Chamber of Commerce, whose membership included Parks Sausage, Supreme Life Insurance Company, Baldwin Advertising, and

Metropolitan Sausage, all successful African American businesses. He gave generously to charities and scholarship funds for African Americans.

In 1984, Fuller sold his business to Dudley. Fuller died on October 24, 1988 of kidney failure. He will continue to be credited with being a trailblazer in business. He was survived by his wife, Lestine Fuller, a backbone of the business. She was the first female salesperson in the company. She died in 1999 at age ninety-one. Their legacy lives on in the success of Dudley Products, Johnson Products, and other African American companies.

Giving Back: S. B. Fuller Mentors George E. Johnson

S. B. Fuller believed in mentoring. He stressed discipline, hard work, and faith to his employees. One of the successful individuals he mentored was George E. Johnson, who became a multimillionaire.

George E. Johnson was born on June 16, 1927 in Richton, Mississippi. He came to Chicago and found work with S. B. Fuller. After working with Fuller, Johnson, at age twenty-seven, used a $500 loan to start the Johnson Products Company. With the help of his wife, Joan Henderson Johnson, Johnson manufactured the company's first hair care product, Ultra Wave hair straightener for men. Other products included Afro Sheen, Gentle Treatment, Ultra Sheen, Sta-Sof-Fro, and Classy Curl.

The company became a multimillion-dollar cosmetics business. In 1971, it was the first African American–owned company to be listed on the American Stock Exchange. Also in 1971, Johnson Products became the first African American advertiser to sponsor a nationally syndicated TV Show, *Soul Train*.

Johnson was dedicated to cultural and civic organizations, including the Chicago Urban League, the Lyric Opera, Northwestern Memorial Hospital, Operation PUSH, and Junior Achievement of Chicago. *Ebony* magazine honored Johnson in 1978 with its American Black Achievement Award. In 1979, Johnson received the public service award of the Harvard Club for the work of the George E. Johnson Foundation and the George E. Johnson Educational Fund.

PART FOUR

◆

MODERN TIMES

JOHN H.
JOHNSON
(B.1918)

John H. Johnson was the first African American to attain major success in magazine publishing. Johnson Publishing Company, Inc., which publishes *Ebony* and *Jet* magazines, is the world's largest African American–owned publishing company. In addition to publishing *Ebony, Jet, Black Star, Black World* and *Ebony Jr.* magazines, the company produces Fashion Fair Cosmetics and the *Ebony* Fashion Fair, as well as books. Johnson started his company in 1942 with money from family and friends. Today, the company has more than three thousand employees and annual sales that exceed $350 million.

Johnson was born Johnny Johnson to John and Gertrude Johnson on January 19, 1918, in a tin-roofed shotgun house in the poor town of Arkansas City, Arkansas. Shotgun houses, generally found in the rural South, were named for the placement of rooms one behind the other. It was said that one could fire a shotgun through the rooms and the shell would go directly through the house. Johnson's father died in a sawmill accident when he was eight years old, and his mother remarried. Arkansas City offered no opportunities for African American prosperity.

The only jobs available were those that required a lot of work for low pay, such as field laborers and maids. Johnson's mother had only completed third grade, and she hoped that her son would go farther in life.

Johnny attended Arkansas City Colored School through the eighth grade. This was the extent of schooling available to blacks in the town and in much of the South. The only option for high school were boarding schools in Pine Bluff or Little Rock, but they were too expensive for the Johnson family. Johnny's mother heard that there were great opportunities for education and employment up north in Chicago. To keep Johnny in school, his mother made him repeat the eighth grade until she saved enough to move to Chicago, where he would receive a better high school education. She worked hard in the fields and kitchens of Arkansas City and finally saved enough money for train tickets to Chicago. But Johnny's stepfather refused to leave. His mother had to make a choice. In 1933, she left her husband behind in Arkansas. Taking few belongings, they boarded a train north to Chicago, joining the Great Migration to that city. Johnny's stepfather later changed his mind and joined them.

When they arrived in Chicago, they did not soon find the better life they were looking for. Jobs were scarce and many black families were huddled together in small spaces. John's mother found temporary work in a clothing factory, but when that job ended the family had to apply for welfare. They were denied at first, so Mrs. Johnson wrote to then president Franklin Roosevelt. Her plea succeeded, and the family was soon given welfare. Her persistence taught young John to not settle for less and to speak up for your rights.

Johnny entered Wendell Phillips High School, an all-black high school, where he was an outstanding student. He loved to read and spent much of his time at the Fifty-eighth Street branch of the Chicago Public Library. Johnny read books by Booker T. Washington and W. E. B. DuBois and some of the first self-help books, especially *How to Win Friends and Influence People* by Dale Carnegie.

BOOKER T. WASHINGTON AND W. E. B. DuBois

Booker T. Washington was born a slave in 1856 in Virginia. Educated at Hampton Institute, Norfolk, Virginia, he began working at Tuskegee Institute in 1881. He built Tuskegee into a center of learning and industrial and agricultural training. Washington believed that blacks should concentrate on developing technical and mechanical skills before actively seeking equality. He strongly believed in entrepreneurship, that blacks should pursue their own economic and moral advancement rather than seek it through legal and political changes.

W. E. B. DuBois was born on February 23, 1868 in Barrington, Massachusetts. He was a leading black intellectual of the twentieth century. In 1905, he founded the Niagara Movement, which became the NAACP in 1909. DuBois took a stand against Booker T. Washington's policy of accommodation, instead calling for an insistent demand for equality. He believed that blacks should cultivate their own cultural values even as they made strides toward social emancipation.

When Wendell Phillips High School burned down, Johnny transferred to the newly constructed Jean Baptiste Pointe Du Sable High School in Chicago, named for an African American fur trader who is credited with founding Chicago. Johnny's classmates included singer Nat "King" Cole, jazz pianist Dorothy Donegan, comedian Redd Foxx, and businessman Dempsey Travis. In high school, other students often teased Johnny about his southern accent. He wanted to change the way he spoke, so he spent hours before a mirror practicing his speech. In a short time, it was no different than the speech of other students. In fact, he was more articulate and had a larger vocabulary than did many of his peers.

While a student at Du Sable, Johnny was active in extracurricular activities, including serving as managing editor of the school paper and business manager of the yearbook. His work in these positions encouraged him to pursue journalism. He was also elected president of his junior and senior classes. One of his teachers at Du Sable High School told him that he needed an adult name, so he stopped calling himself Johnny and began to use John instead. In addition, he gave himself the middle name of Harold, and after that he was known as John H. Johnson.

Johnson graduated from Du Sable in 1936. He was the only student selected to speak at the commencement. After graduating, Johnson had the good fortune to meet Harry H. Pace, president of the Supreme Liberty Life Insurance Company. This meeting changed his life and directed his path to success. After high school, Johnson worked with the National Youth Administration. He also worked at the Supreme Liberty Life Insurance Company, where he earned $25 a month. Mary McLeod Bethune, a strong role model and influence in his life, helped him get a scholarship to the University of Chicago, where Johnson planned to study law while continuing to work at Supreme Life Insurance Company. Bethune was an educator and founder of the Daytona Normal and Industrial School for Negro Girls (now named Bethune-Cookman College). Bethune was a part of President Franklin D. Roosevelt's "Black Cabinet," a group of African American advisors.

Johnson decided to drop out of college, however, as opportunities opened up at the company for him. Harry H. Pace was so impressed with the young man that he made Johnson editor of the company's newspaper. As part of his job, Johnson was required to collect positive news stories about African Americans. He came up with an ingenious idea of putting together a magazine that would feature upbeat articles about African Americans. He chose the name *Negro Digest*.

Johnson used his mother's furniture as security for a $500 loan. According to Jim Haskins's in *African American Entrepreneurs*, Johnson "mailed 20,000 copies of a letter offering charter subscriptions to his new magazine. Three thousand people sent in the $2 annual subscription fee, giving Johnson $6,000 to start his venture." In 1942, the first issue of *Negro Digest* sold three thousand copies. Its publication was met with enthusiasm and support from African Americans. This success convinced Johnson that there was a need and a market for his new magazine. By late 1943, the circulation for the magazine jumped from fifty thousand to one hundred thousand.

Johnson married Eunice Wright in 1941. In 1943, Johnson purchased his first building. He also bought a three-story apartment for his family, including his mother, who was on his staff for many years. In 1945, Johnson conceived the idea for a pictorial magazine for African Americans to meet what he foresaw was a tremendous need for positive news about and depictions of African Americans. Johnson's wife Eunice suggested the name *Ebony* for the magazine, which is a black wood found in Africa. The first printing of twenty-five thousand copies sold out within a few hours. Millions of African Americans as well as whites have read the magazine over the years. It has served a special purpose in instilling pride, informing readers about current events, and presenting history that has escaped the pages of mainstream publications.

The only competitor to *Ebony* was a magazine called *Our World*. That magazine eventually went bankrupt and Johnson purchased it for $14,000. As part of the deal, he hired Moneta Sleet Jr. who would become the premier photographer at *Ebony* for many years. Sleet became the first African American photographer to be awarded a Pulitzer Prize for the touching photo of Coretta Scott King and her children at Martin Luther King Jr.'s funeral.

Johnson and his wife have shared their wealth with charities, colleges, and universities. The *Ebony* Fashion Fair, coordinated by Johnson's wife, has donated more than $49 million to the United Negro College Fund and other charities since it began in 1958. In January 2003, Johnson contributed $4 million to Howard University, one of the largest gifts it has ever received. Howard is renaming its school of communication for this publishing magnate.

John H. Johnson has received numerous awards for his achievements. He was among a group of distinguished Chicagoans who were honored by the Chicago Historical Society for the significant roles they have played in helping shape the city and its history. In February 2001, he was inducted into the Arkansas Business Hall of Fame, and in 2002 Johnson received an honorary doctor of law degree at the University of Arkansas.

CRISPUS ATTUCKS
WRIGHT

(1913–2001)

The son of a former slave in Louisiana, Crispus Attucks Wright rose from selling newspapers to becoming a man of wealth and influence. In 1997, Wright, a successful Los Angeles lawyer, gave $2 million to his alma mater, the University of Southern California (USC) Law Center, to establish scholarships in his name. Wright's scholarships would be awarded to minority law students and others dedicated to practice in underserved minority communities. At the time, Wright's gift to the USC Law School was the school's largest gift by an African American. Discussing his philanthropy in the *Los Angeles Times* Wright said, "We stand on the shoulders of hundreds who sacrificed and paved the way for us, and what better way to repay those wonderful souls than to give something back."

Wright was born in Louisiana in 1913, the fiftieth anniversary of the Emancipation Proclamation. His father Warner Wright named him after Crispus Attucks, a free African American seaman who was the first man to be killed in the Revolutionary War.

Wright's father was a powerful influence in young Crispus's life.

He believed in the power of education to change a person. Twenty-five years after slavery ended, Warner Wright graduated from Leland University, one of several institutions that made it possible for African Americans in segregated New Orleans to receive a college education. After graduating from college, Wright's father served as a teacher and a school principal in segregated Louisiana schools.

When Crispus was a young child, the Wright family moved to California in search of better jobs and educational opportunities for their children. When young Crispus was five years old, his father died. His mother worked hard as a janitor and maid to support her family. She never complained, there was no time to with eight children to be fed, clothed, and educated.

One day, young Crispus met W. E. B. DuBois, who was attending an NAACP convention in Los Angeles. This meeting would be the beginning of Wright's interest in the struggle for equal opportunity for blacks. Throughout high school, Wright was an excellent student and won recognition for his abilities as a debater at Manual Arts High School in Los Angeles. After school he often walked to the courthouse to listen to Attorney Willis O. Tyler and his young partner, Edwin L. Jefferson, a 1931 USC Law School graduate. These figures inspired and encouraged Wright to pursue law and enroll at USC.

Wright's mother achieved her goal of providing for and educating her children. Thanks to her hard work and determination, seven of her eight children graduated from college. Three of them studied at USC: Warner II, who became a physician, Mercedes, and Crispus.

Wright enrolled in USC in 1932 at the height of the Depression. Due to the Great Depression, Wright transferred to the University of California, Los Angeles (UCLA) on Vermont Avenue. After two years at UCLA, Wright returned to USC and earned a Bachelor of Arts degree in 1936. He set his sights on attending the USC Law School. Wright was the only black when he attended USC Law School, pursuing his dream while holding down two jobs, and graduated with a law degree in 1938.

After law school, Wright was faced with the problem of any young lawyer: he had to convince clients that he could handle their cases. At the same time, he had to persuade black clients that they would get the same kind of representation that white lawyers would offer them. When Wright graduated from law school, he was unable to join the Los Angeles Bar Association because he was African American. Consequently, in 1943, he founded the John W. Langston Bar Association, which became the most prominent black legal association in Los Angeles. As part of this association, Wright helped the NAACP prepare briefs in the 1940s that led to a U.S. Supreme Court ruling that struck down restrictive real estate contracts as unconstitutional. This association, which met at the Club Alabama next to the Hotel Somerville, was a professional forum for the local African American legal community. One of its primary goals was to deal with discrimination.

When Wright's family moved to California, the only place where they could buy a home was in South Los Angeles. At the time there were laws called restrictive covenants that prevented African Americans from buying homes in many Los Angeles neighborhoods. Wright was determined to change this discriminatory policy. He helped a group of attorneys representing the NAACP prepare a legal fight against restrictive covenants. They won the case when the U.S. Supreme Court ruled in the late 1940s that restrictive real estate covenants were

DUNBAR HOTEL

This hotel was originally called the Somerville, named for its founder, Dr. John Alexander Somerville, a business and cultural leader, and his wife Vada, both graduates of the USC dental school. Somerville and his wife were denied lodging on an early trip to California. He vowed to build a hotel where African Americans would be welcome, and made good on his promise in 1928.

unconstitutional. Consequently, he built his home in the affluent area of Country Club Park, despite neighbors pressuring him not to build there.

While Wright was practicing law, he also became the owner of a profitable Los Angeles mortuary and eight convenience stores. He also invested in the *Los Angeles Sentinel*, the oldest continually published African American newspaper in the West.

Wright's $2 million gift to USC, to provide scholarships for needy students, was prompted by the recent ban on affirmative action programs at California colleges and universities. He did so also remembering his own financial struggle and a $50 scholarship that made such a difference in his life.

Wright died on December 4, 2001, in Los Angeles. He was eighty-seven. Widowed in 1979, Wright lost his only son in 2001. He is survived by a grandson, Warner Richard Wright IV, and a sister, Miriam Lee.

MATEL "MAT"
DAWSON JR.

(1922–2002)

Mat Dawson, a rigger at Ford Motor Company's Rouge Complex in Dearborn, Michigan, knew about hard work, sheer will, and determination. As a rigger, he used cranes and cables to move items throughout the plant. Dawson would rise before 5 A.M. to go to his shift. He stayed with Ford all of his life, and over the years this man who had only an eighth-grade education donated more than $1 million to educational institutions and agencies.

Most people retire at around age sixty-five, but Mat Dawson continued working into his eighties. When Dawson finally retired, he was the oldest worker at Ford. He was also one of the most highly respected, both by management and his fellow workers. He would not have known what to do if he didn't continue working, he said, surrounded by coworkers who had become like family.

Matel Dawson, the third youngest of six brothers and a sister, was born on January 3, 1921. He grew up in Shreveport, Louisiana. His father was a groundskeeper who worked his way up to head cook at the Tri-State Sanitarium, and his mother took in laundry to help

FORD MOTOR COMPANY

Henry Ford, the founder of Ford Motor Company, built his first car in Detroit in 1896. By the late 1930s, Detroit had a population of over 175,000 African Americans, who settled primarily on the east side of town near the car factories. Ford became a major employer of African Americans.

support the family. Dawson left school after eighth grade. At the time, his destiny would have been to work for minimum wages and live in poverty with little or no chance for wealth. Dawson did not accept this destiny. He knew that he could overcome a limited education through hard work, a desire to improve his economic conditions, and a strong will to make significant contributions to the world.

In 1939, Dawson left Shreveport and went to Detroit to join an uncle who worked for Ford Motor Company. Dawson was excited about living in Detroit. Many African Americans there were doing well economically. There was a special spirit of pride in the air among them, as boxer Joe Louis held the heavyweight boxing crown off and on between 1935 and 1949. Ford offered Dawson $1.25 an hour, which he considered to be a good wage, more money than Dawson could have ever dreamed of making in Shreveport at the time.

Dawson's road to accumulating wealth began around 1940, when he began making a habit of saving money. He diligently saved $25 a week out of each paycheck. As his wages increased, Dawson saved more money. He credited his mother with teaching him the importance of saving. His mother taught him that all people can accumulate wealth if they make an effort to save and invest their money. While Dawson could have splurged on many things, he chose to live within his means, the amount of money he set aside for his living expenses. He lived in a small apartment and drove Ford cars. When Dawson was married, he purchased a home with a thirty-year mortgage. But he did not like the lengthy payment plan and paid off the mortgage within six years. At Ford, Dawson routinely worked seven days a week, often working a double shift to get as much overtime as possible.

Dawson believed that there was no better way to use his money than to help someone get an education. He helped a number of students pursue and complete their college degrees. Over ten years, Dawson contributed $640,000 to Wayne State University in Detroit, $400,000 to Louisiana State University, and $230,000 to the United Negro College Fund. These scholarships, in honor of his parents and grandparents, provide full four-year tuition to deserving students.

Mat Dawson lived a frugal life, spending little on material things and avoiding the use of credit cards. While earning more than $100,000 a year at Ford, he put more than 75 percent of his income into savings. He also invested in stocks, bonds, mutual funds, and real estate. As an employee at Ford Motors, he took advantage of the stock options, which increased his wealth and ability to give away millions.

Dawson received many honors during his lifetime: Former President Bill Clinton recognized him for his generosity. The National Urban League, the International Heritage Hall of Fame, and the United Negro College Fund also honored him. Numerous television stations and magazines, including CBS, NBC, and ABC, and *Parade, Jet,* and *Ebony* magazines, profiled Dawson. Louisiana State University at Shreveport awarded Dawson an honorary Doctor of Humane Letters degree at the spring 2000 commencement, and he received another honorary doctorate from Wayne State University in Detroit. The state of Michigan chose him as its "Michiganian of the Year" in 1991.

Three years after his retirement from the Ford Motor Company Rouge Complex in Dearborn, Michigan, Dawson died on November 2, 2002, at his Highland Park, Michigan, home. He was eighty-one. Before his death, Dawson ordered a customized crypt from India and decided that his epitaph should read: "Mat Dawson Jr.—Gone but not forgotten."

JONES

(B. 1933)

Quincy Jones is one of the most celebrated artists in the world. His more than a half-century of contributions to music and his support of other artists is unsurpassed. Jones has made his mark as an arranger, performer, music producer, entrepreneur, and humanitarian. His contributions to music have made him one of the most powerful individuals in the entertainment industry.

Quincy Delight Jones Jr. was born on March 14, 1933, in Chicago, the son of Quincy Delight Jones Sr. and Sarah Jones. His parents, like many other African Americans at the time, moved from South Carolina to Chicago in search of better jobs, educational opportunities, and freedom. Upon arriving in Chicago, the Jones family was faced with difficulties. Sarah Jones suffered from mental illness and was institutionalized or under the care of a doctor for most of her life. This caused considerable stress and hardship on the family. Shortly after their younger son Lloyd was born, Quincy Sr. and his wife divorced.

Quincy Jr. showed an aptitude for music and began playing the piano at an early age. While he lived in Chicago, he and his father

enjoyed going to hear music on the South Side. Jones was influenced by the musicians he heard at these South Side clubs, such as Lionel Hampton, Count Basie, and others. He knew early in life that he would become a musician. Lionel Hampton would later help launch Jones's music career.

After his divorce, Quincy Sr. remarried and moved his family to Bremerton, Washington, a town outside Seattle. The extended family consisted of his new wife Elvira, her three children from a previous marriage, and his two sons. In 1948, the family moved to Seattle, which was considered to be the music capital of the Pacific Northwest, where Quincy began to show a greater interest in music. He took music classes in elementary and secondary school. Quincy was active in music in high school, where he played the piano and joined the high school band, becoming its student manager. In church, he organized a choir. He played a variety of instruments, including the baritone saxophone, clarinet, trombone, tuba, trumpet, and French horn. He was also involved in the high school orchestra, dance band, and chorus.

Quincy wrote his first composition in high school, a suite called *From the Four Winds*. It was an impressive accomplishment for someone who had not been trained in composition or advanced theory. It caught the attention of Lionel Hampton, who was performing in Seattle. After hearing the piece, Hampton offered Quincy an opportunity to join his band. But Quincy did not join at the time because Lionel Hampton's wife felt that he was too young and should finish high school first.

While living in Seattle, Quincy made the rounds of clubs, listening to such great musicians as Cab Calloway, Billie Holiday, Count Basie, Clark Terry, the Duke Ellington Orchestra, Dizzy Gillespie, and Charlie Parker. The teenager soaked up all of this richness and was convinced that his life would be filled with making, arranging, and producing music.

Around 1950, Quincy Jones also was influenced by Ray Charles, who had moved to Seattle for musical opportunities. Charles was proficient in arranging and composing music, and he also demonstrated remarkable versatility in that he could play the alto saxophone, clarinet, piano, and organ. He taught young Quincy how to arrange music, with special emphasis on arranging for big jazz bands and writing polytones. In addition, Charles taught his protege how to read and write in braille. Their special relationship would last a lifetime and they were each influenced by the other in their musical careers.

In 1950, Jones finished high school and won two scholarships to study music, one at the University of Washington in Seattle and the other at Schillinger's House of Music, the renowned Boston institution, which is now the Berklee College of Music. He chose Schillinger's. Jones excelled in his intensive classes at this college. At night, he was drawn to the clubs where he sometimes played. On weekends, Jones and his college buddies would head for New York, where they had many opportunities to hear such jazz greats as Charlie Parker, Thelonious Monk, Charles Mingus, and Art Tatum.

Shortly after Jones's eighteenth birthday, Lionel Hampton approached him again about joining his band. Jones left college and began playing with Hampton as an arranger, pianist, and trumpeter. His stint with Hampton lasted from 1951 to 1959.

Upon his return to the United States from a European tour in 1953, Jones set his sights on recording. He began freelance arranging for jazz and commercial recordings. Jones's clients included James Cleveland, Lavern Baker, Chuck Willis, Dinah Washington, Johnny Mathis, and Lionel Hampton.

By 1956, Jones had begun to be recognized more widely for his musical talent. He received the New Star Arranger award in the *Encyclopedia of Jazz* poll. That same year he had the special opportunity to arrange music for a band led by the great trumpeter Dizzy Gillespie.

Along the way, Irving Green, the president of Mercury Records, offered Jones the position of staff arranger. He took the job, and while at Mercury, Jones was able to arrange an album for ABC-Paramount featuring his friend Ray Charles. Jones rose to the position of vice president at Mercury, becoming the first African American executive at a major label in the recording industry. He won his first Grammy in 1963 for Count Basie's arrangement of Ray Charles's *I Can't Stop Loving You*. His talent was also apparent in his production of Lesley Gore's album, *I'll Cry If I Want To,* which sold over 10 million copies in 1963.

While Jones had many successes at Mercury and enjoyed his influential position, he longed to fulfill his dream of scoring sound tracks for movies. In 1965, he left Mercury Records and moved to Hollywood where he would have greater access to the film industry. His first major sound track was for Sidney Lumet's film *The Pawnbroker*. A year later, Jones did the sound track for the film *Mirage*.

Jones had more requests for doing sound tracks than he could complete. Some of his successful sound tracks include *In Cold Blood, In the Heat of the Night*, and *For the Love of Ivy*. In addition to movie sound tracks, Jones wrote music for the television shows *Ironside* and *The Bill Cosby Show*.

Over time, Jones began producing his own albums. His first album, *Walking in Space,* was with A&M Records. Jones received a Grammy for best performance by a large group in 1969. In 1970, he produced a follow-up album, *Gula Matari*, which also won a Grammy for best instrumental composition and best instrumental arrangement.

One of the best-known albums by Quincy Jones was *Body Heat,* which was produced in 1974. The album was an instant success, selling more than a million copies in the United States. Although it was a good year for him musically, Quincy faced a serious emergency with a cerebral stroke brought on by a ruptured aneurysm. He underwent surgery and surgeons found a second aneurysm on the opposite side of his brain. Another surgery was performed, and within a year, Quincy was back to his music.

Jones was also the producer of recordings by Michael Jackson, Tevin Campbell, Keith Washington, Ernestine Anderson, the Winans, and many others. One of his most successful ventures was the collaboration with Michael Jackson to produce *Thriller*, which sold more than 40 million copies, making it the best-selling album in recording history.

Jones has received many awards for his great contributions to music and film, including seven Oscar nominations. Jones is the recipient of 27 Grammy awards, more than any other living recording artist. Over the years, Jones has received some seventy-nine Grammy nominations. He has also received many honorary doctorates from colleges and universities, including Howard, Harvard, Tuskegee, New York University, Berklee College of Music, and the University of Miami. Awards for Jones have come from many countries, including France, Switzerland, Germany, and England. His mentoring has helped countless musicians rise to fame and fortune.

Along the way, Quincy Jones began to share his wealth to help others. In 1985, he pulled together forty of the best recording stars to record *We Are the World* to raise money to feed the victims of Ethiopia's drought and famine.

The Quincy Jones Listen Up Foundation supports programs that meet the health care and educational needs of children. The foundation works to bridge the gap between privilege and poverty for young people around the world. Jones continues to place his mark on pop, soul, hip-hop, jazz, classical, African, and Brazilian music. In 1997, Jones formed the Quincy Jones Media Group (QJMG). Through this company, he is developing various projects for film, television, and the Internet.

EARL G.
GRAVES

(B. 1935)

Earl Graves is considered an authority on black business. He is the founder of *Black Enterprise* magazine, which has a circulation of more than five hundred thousand, that he founded to inspire African Americans to get into business and to teach them to thrive. *Black Enterprise* is considered the most important resource for African American business professionals, entrepreneurs, and policy makers in the public and private sectors. Graves is also co-owner with Earvin "Magic" Johnson of a Washington, D.C.–based Pepsi Cola distributorship, the largest minority-controlled Pepsi franchise in the country.

Earl Gilbert Graves was born on January 9, 1935, in Brooklyn, New York, to Earl Godwin Graves and Winifred Sealy Graves. He was raised in a neighborhood called Bedford-Stuyvesant, where he learned hard work, discipline, and perseverance from his West Indian parents. Graves's parents stressed the importance of education, and Earl learned that lesson well. He was a good and attentive student in elementary school. Earl began using his talent from business when he was five years old. He sold Christmas cards and was honored for

being the top seller. At Erasmus High School, Earl was an excellent student and also excelled as a track star.

After graduating from Erasmus, Earl entered Morgan State University. He was an outstanding student, making the dean's list, running several campus businesses, and was also a member of the Reserve Officers Training Corps (ROTC). He graduated in 1958 with a Bachelor of Arts degree in economics and was commissioned as a second lieutenant in the U. S. Army. During his two-year stint of military service, Graves completed Airborne and Ranger School and was promoted to the rank of captain.

In 1960, Graves married Barbara Kydd of Brooklyn. In 1962 he began working as a narcotics agent with the U. S. Treasury Department. When he finished this assignment, he returned to his old neighborhood in Brooklyn and ventured into selling and developing real estate. He decided to try something different and started working in politics as an assistant on the staff of then Senator Robert F. Kennedy. The senator, who was a strong supporter of civil rights, was campaigning to become president.

Senator Kennedy was assassinated in 1968. It was a difficult time for the country, which had already undergone the death by assassination of Martin Luther King Jr., Malcolm X, and Senator Kennedy's brother, President John F. Kennedy. Graves had to cope with the tragedy both personally and professionally, including figuring out a new direction for his career. After several months of reflection, Graves decided to enter the business arena. He remembered that his father had always taught him the importance of developing a strong economic base in the African American community. Consequently, he founded Earl G. Graves Associates, a consulting firm that provided assistance to corporations on urban affairs and economic development.

Graves received a Ford Foundation grant to study black-owned business in the Caribbean. By 1970, Graves embarked on a venture to publish a monthly digest, which would include news, commentary, and informative articles about African American business.

A catalog about the proposed *Black Enterprise* magazine was presented to possible lenders. Graves managed to get several thousand letters of support for his magazine. In 1970, Graves borrowed $150,000 from the Manhattan Capital Corporation of Chase Manhattan bank and the magazine began publication. It began to turn a profit after its tenth issue, with more than $900,000 in advertising revenues. In 1972, Graves began featuring a list of top black businesses, which has become an annual feature and the top-selling issue of *Black Enterprise*. The magazine has been successful because it appeals to many people interested in business, and its articles on investment, political issues, health, and technology make it a valuable source of information.

The entire Graves family is involved in the Earl G. Graves Publishing Company.

Graves's wife, Barbara, left teaching to become a full partner with her husband. She now serves as vice president and general manager of the Earl G. Graves Publishing Company. All three sons are involved as well. Earl Jr., the eldest, has a degree from Yale and an M.B.A. from the Harvard Business School. He was drafted by the Philadelphia 76ers basketball team, but decided to join his father in business instead. John, the second son, is a graduate of Brown University and Yale Law School. He serves as vice president of business ventures and legal affairs for the company. Michael, the youngest son, works in his father's Pepsi Cola franchise as a development manager.

Graves is active in many organizations and has received numerous awards for his work. He once served as National Commissioner of Scouting for the Boy Scouts of America. He is one of the 100 Most Influential Blacks listed in *Ebony*. His support of historically African American colleges and universities has earned him honorary doctorates from Rust College, Lincoln University, Morehouse College, Morgan State University, Hampton University, and Meharry Medical College.

Although Graves has a busy work schedule, he finds time to serve as a member of the board of directors of the Rohm and Haas Corporation, the New York State Urban Development Corporation, the Chrysler Corporation, and the Magazine Publishers Association. He also has membership in such organizations as the NAACP, Sigma Pi Phi, and the Visiting Committee of Harvard University's John F. Kennedy School of Government.

JOE L.
DUDLEY SR.

(B . 1 9 3 7)

As early as first grade, Joe L. Dudley's teachers treated his speech impediment as a reason to label him mentally retarded and to treat him differently than the other children. But Joe's mother knew he should not be in special education classes. She knew he could achieve and constantly told her son that he was smart and no different from any other child. Her love and support encouraged Joe to study hard and become a wealthy man. Dudley, who was born "dirt poor," made his first million before he was forty years old. Today, he is worth nearly $400 million.

Through a strong sense of self, Joe L. Dudley became the president and chief executive officer (CEO) of Dudley Products, Inc., one of the largest manufacturers and distributors of beauty and hair care products. His company has become a training facility, offering cosmetologists advanced training in hair and beauty care.

Joe was born on May 9, 1937, the fifth of eleven children born to Gilmer L. Dudley and Clara Yeates Dudley, in Aurora, North Carolina. He and his siblings lived in a simple three-room farmhouse. Joe's

mother encouraged him throughout elementary and secondary school. He achieved in his schoolwork and slowly overcame the shyness he felt because of his speech impediment.

After finishing high school, Joe became a student at North Carolina Agricultural and Technical State University in Greensboro. While still a student, he took on a part-time job selling Fuller Products, including cosmetics and soaps, door-to-door. Starting with $10 to buy the first products, Dudley was on his journey to becoming a successful and prosperous businessman.

He would not let any kind of discrimination determine his fate. Dudley spent his summer breaks from college working full time for Fuller Products in Brooklyn. The seed for his future company, Dudley Products, Inc., was planted that first summer. Senior representatives for the company recognized his business ability. After graduating from college with a Bachelor of Science in business administration, Dudley returned to Brooklyn and began working full time for Fuller Products.

In 1960, Dudley met Eunice Mosley, who was also selling Fuller Products to earn college tuition. They fell in love and married in 1961. The Dudleys began working full time with Fuller Products in 1962. Sometime later, they met and worked with S. B. Fuller himself, the owner of Fuller Products, and one of the most successful African American entrepreneurs. Mr. Fuller became their mentor, and the Dudleys were on their way to creating their own company.

In 1967, Dudley became one of the youngest employees to open a Fuller distributorship in Greensboro, North Carolina, where he had spent his college years, had established a good reputation as a college student, and made many friends and professional contacts. Within a few years, Dudley's distributorship became one of the company's top performers.

Ingenuity served Dudley well in his business venture. He and his family made their own packaging when Fuller Products Company experienced problems supplying them. When demand outweighed supply, Dudley had a novel idea: He would use the kitchen as a laboratory, packaging products in old mayonnaise jars, jelly jars, and empty containers from beauty operators and other businesses. This creativity served as the foundation for a future full-fledged company laboratory.

In 1975, Dudley opened the Dudley Products Company. Within a year, the company had more than four hundred employees. Dudley, much like his mentor S. B. Fuller, had other business interests, including a chain of hair care and beauty supply stores and a beauty school. His success was recognized nationally and soon made him one of the most influential African Americans in the country. Dudley products are distributed to and used by thousands of cosmetologists.

By 1976, S. B. Fuller was seventy-one and in failing health, no longer able to effectively run the corporation he founded. Fuller wanted to find someone who would operate his business. He immediately thought of Dudley and made an offer to him to move to Chicago and become president of the Fuller Products Corporation. Dudley accepted, glad to work once more with the man who had helped give him his start in business. He moved to Chicago and managed both the Fuller Company and the Dudley Company with excellence. By age forty, Dudley had become a millionaire.

Dudley operated the two businesses until 1984, when he purchased the rights to the Fuller Products Company and returned to North Carolina to run Dudley Products. His business continued to grow and soon became recognized by *Black Enterprise* as one of the top fifty African American businesses. For more than thirty-three years, this multimillionaire's company has flourished under the joint leadership of Dr. Joe L. Dudley Sr. and his wife, Dr. Eunice Mosley Dudley. (The Dudleys received honorary doctorates from North Carolina A&T University and Edward Waters College in Florida.) The company has become one of the largest manufacturers and distributors of ethnic hair-care products and cosmetics in the United States.

Throughout the years of success of his company, Dudley has always given back. Dudley has paid for 125 students to get a Bachelor of Science degree at North Carolina A&T University. He mentors youth and spends much of his time giving motivational speeches across the country. He shares stories of being labeled and treated as mentally retarded. Dudley appeals to the members of his audience to aim high and never use the labels of others to define them. He challenges people to maximize their potential and achieve success.

Dudley also developed the Dudley Collegiate Program, which identifies and works with college students interested in developing selling, business, and leadership skills. Scholarships are made available to high school seniors through the Dudley Scholarship Program.

Dudley has also been elected to the Horatio Alger Association of distinguished Americans. He has received numerous awards, including the North Carolina A&T Alumni Excellence Award and the Maya Angelou Tribute to Achievement Award, and he was inducted into the National Black College Alumni Hall of Fame.

The Dudleys are the parents of three children, all involved in the family business. Mrs. Dudley serves as the chief financial officer and executive director of the Dudley Beauty School System. Joe Jr., who holds an undergraduate and Master of Business Administration (MBA) degree from Northwestern University, is vice president of finance. Daughter Ursula, a graduate of Harvard University, serves as director of Dudley Cosmetics, general counsel, and vice president of marketing. Genea, the younger daughter, a graduate of Duke University who holds a MBA, is brand manager in the corporation.

Ed and Bettiann Gardner, Innovators in African American Hair Care

Ed and Bettiann Gardner recognized that many of the mainstream hair care companies did not provide appropriate products for people of color. They wanted to change that and founded Soft Sheen Products in 1964. Much like Joe Dudley, they began with a small family operation. They used the basement of their home in Chicago to develop, package, and market their products.

Soft Sheen Products soon grew into a multimillion-dollar enterprise employing over four hundred Chicagoans. The popular products were sold throughout the country and exported to Canada, West Africa, and the Caribbean. The L'Oreal group purchased Soft Sheen Products in 1998.

Ed and Bettiann Gardner are also part owners of the Chicago Bulls and members of the board of directors of *Black Enterprise* magazine. The Gardners have always been supporters of the arts and African American theater. In 1987, they helped bring back the legendary Regal Theater in Chicago by contributing millions for a new building.

REGINALD FRANCIS
LEWIS
(1942–1993)

Reginald Lewis was a businessman at an early age. As a nine-year old, he started delivering papers in his East Baltimore, Maryland, neighborhood. He did so well, he sold his newspaper route to another boy. Young Reginald set a goal as a child to become one of the richest men in the world, a dream that he would eventually achieve. His personal fortune was estimated to exceed $400 million. He became the first African American businessman to make *Forbes* magazine's list of the nation's 400 wealthiest individuals.

Lewis purchased the Beatrice International Food Company in 1987 for $985 million. Within five years, the corporation had sales that exceeded $1.6 billion. The Reginald Lewis Foundation has contributed millions of dollars to charities, colleges, and cultural institutions.

Reginald Francis Lewis was born on December 7, 1942, in Baltimore, to Clinton and Carolyn Cooper Lewis. He grew up in East Baltimore, the only section of the city where African Americans lived and worked in Baltimore. Prior to the Civil War, slaves were brought in chains to East Baltimore and placed on ships for slave auctions in

New Orleans. East Baltimore was where the abolitionist Frederick Douglass, a former slave, witnessed the slave trade and made a commitment to free all slaves in the country.

Lewis's parents instilled in him values about the importance of hard work and the understanding that nothing in life was free. He attended St. Francis Xavier School from kindergarten through eighth grade. Young Reginald was a good student, but he felt that some of the nuns could be too strict. Throughout elementary and secondary school, he was a high achiever and he was excited about going to Dunbar High School. Named for the poet Paul Laurence Dunbar, it was an all-black school. Although it did not have the facilities, equipment, and resources of white schools, it was staffed with a highly educated and caring faculty.

Lewis worked at a Baltimore country club in the summers, and excelled in academics and sports during the school year. As captain of the football, basketball, and baseball teams in high school, Lewis's goal was to become a professional athlete and later start a career in law or business. After completing high school, Lewis enrolled at Virginia State University (VSU) on scholarship. While at VSU, he played as quarterback of the football team until a shoulder injury sidelined him, ending his goal of becoming a professional football player.

The university had a highly talented faculty that challenged all students to reach their maximum potential. Besides being mentors and teachers to African American students, many on the faculty were regarded as surrogate parents by the students. While at VSU, Lewis became interested in economics and its relationship to everyday people.

After college, Lewis focused on law school. Having graduated at the top of his class at VSU, he was confident about being accepted. Although Lewis was interested in business and economics, he chose law after participating in a summer minority program at Harvard Law School. His professors were quite impressed with him and encouraged Lewis to pursue law rather than business. The only question was where he would attend. One of his college professors had challenged him to choose the best law school in the country. Harvard University was widely recognized for its outstanding law school, so Lewis applied to Harvard and was quickly accepted.

With hard work and discipline, Lewis finished law school with honors. In 1968 he joined the prestigious law firm of Paul, Weiss, Rifkind, Wharton & Garrison in New York City. He remained with the firm for five years and then started his own, the Lewis and Clarkson Law Firm, which became very profitable.

Following his dream of becoming a business leader, Lewis founded the TLC Group. One of the first ventures of TLC was to buy out the McCall Company, the oldest U. S. pattern company. He bought the company in 1983 for $1 million and $28 million in debt. Four years later, Lewis sold the company for $63 million, pocketing $50 million. The profits from this and other business investments allowed Lewis in 1987 to pull off one of the biggest business deals in history with the purchase of Beatrice International Foods for $985 million. It distributed such well-known brands as Butterball turkeys, Good Humor ice cream, and Clark candy bars. Beatrice, one of the largest food businesses in the world, became the largest African American–owned company in the world, with sixty-one companies and markets in thirty-one countries. Its reported sales in 1992 were $1.6 billion.

Reginald Lewis's rise to wealth is attributed to his business acumen, strong will, and financial and legal savvy. When he sought to buy Beatrice International Foods, Lewis outbid several multinational companies, which had a large team of accountants, lawyers, and financial advisers. He singlehandedly pulled off the deal.

Along the way, Lewis continued to reach out to others through his caring philanthropy. He donated $3 million to Harvard University and $1 million to Howard University.

Lewis married Loida Nicolas on August 16, 1969, in a lavish wedding in the heart of Manila, the Philippines, her native country. Loida, a lawyer, became a general attorney with the Immigration and Naturalization Service.

Reginald Lewis passed away in 1993 from brain cancer at the youthful age of 50. His untimely death shocked the world. The significance of this man's life is remembered through the Reginald Lewis Foundation, Inc. It continues to make gifts to institutions that serve all people. In July 2002, a gift of $5 million was given to the proposed Maryland Museum of African American History and Culture (scheduled to open in 2005). This is the largest gift ever given to an African American museum. In honor of Lewis's philanthropy, the museum is named the Reginald F. Lewis Museum of Maryland African American History and Culture.

Lewis is survived by his wife, Loida, and daughters, Leslie Lourdes and Christina Savilla. His estate, worth $84.2 million, was left to his wife and kin. Today, Loida is the chair of the Reginald F. Lewis Foundation.

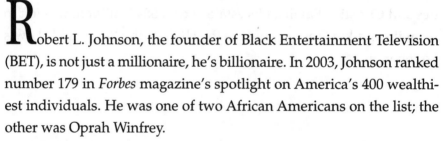

ROBERT L.
JOHNSON
(B. 1946)

♦

Robert L. Johnson, the founder of Black Entertainment Television (BET), is not just a millionaire, he's billionaire. In 2003, Johnson ranked number 179 in *Forbes* magazine's spotlight on America's 400 wealthiest individuals. He was one of two African Americans on the list; the other was Oprah Winfrey.

Johnson overcame obstacles to achieve success, but he believes that obstacles can always be overcome. Johnson's success began with a dream, which he never abandoned.

Robert L. Johnson was born in the small town of Hickory, Mississippi, in 1946, the ninth of ten children born to Archie and Edna Johnson. His mother was a schoolteacher and his father chopped and sold timber on land owned by his great-grandfather Filmore, a freed slave. The Johnson family, like many other African American families in the South, sought a better life in the North. They boarded an Illinois Central train and moved to Freeport, Illinois, a predominantly white, working-class town of factories surrounded by dairy farms. There, the Johnsons found employment. His father supplemented his factory-job income by operating a junkyard and working as a janitor.

As a young boy, Johnson worked mowing yards, delivering newspapers, and doing chores around the house. His free time was spent playing basketball at an old community center on the predominantly black east side of town.

Johnson's parents instilled the value of education in their children at an early age. Young Robert was a gifted student throughout elementary and secondary school. At Freeport High School, he was an honor student and was highly regarded by his teachers and peers. As a high achiever, he knew he would go to college and make his mark in the business world. He had visions of becoming an executive of a large corporation. This vision would materialize later in life when he became a successful and influential businessman.

After high school, Johnson enrolled in the University of Illinois and pursued a major in political science. He graduated in 1968. While at Illinois, Johnson met Sheila Crump, the daughter of a successful doctor. They were married in 1969.

With his goal of becoming an entrepreneur in mind, he entered Princeton University on a full scholarship. Johnson studied at the university's Woodrow Wilson School of Public and International Affairs, a two-year program for students who wanted a career in public service.

It was at Princeton that Johnson recognized the importance of television and its benefits to African Americans and businessmen. In 1972, Johnson completed a Master's degree in public administration. He considered a career in the diplomatic corps but decided to pursue other career opportunities instead. He and Sheila moved to Washington, D.C. His first job there was with the Corporation for Public Broadcasting, followed by a stint at the Washington Urban League.

While he enjoyed his positions in Washington, Johnson's greatest desire was to be involved in television. His dream was to establish a cable company.

In 1976, Johnson began work as a lobbyist for the National Cable

Television Association (NCTA). This position provided experience and knowledge about an industry that would completely revolutionize television. His dream came to fruition in 1978, when at age thirty-two he developed a plan that would lead to wealth and influence.

Johnson and a colleague met with Rep. Claude Pepper of Florida to present a proposal for cable television for the elderly. Pepper did not accept the plan. Johnson revised it to make it a station for African American viewers. To implement this plan, Johnson needed financial backing. He received $15,000 of start-up money from Tom Wheeler, president of the National Cable Television Association (NCTA), and $500,000 from John Malone, the president of Tele-Communications, Inc. While at the 1979 NCTA convention Johnson had the good fortune to meet with a major player at NCTA, Bob Rosencrans, a vice president.

Rosencrans made an offer Johnson could not refuse: Rosencrans needed additional programs for his local cable networks, and he allowed Johnson to use the available slots for his new channel. On January 8, 1980, Black Entertainment Television was founded. The first show on BET was the 1974 movie, *Visit to a Chief's Son*. This program reached 3.8 million homes.

In 1991, BET was the first black-controlled company listed on the New York Stock Exchange (NYSE). BET's $9 million enterprise grew to $475 million in its first day on the NYSE, and Johnson's personal wealth grew to more than $104 million dollars.

The company moved to a new $15 million headquarters in Washington, D. C., in 1995. That year Johnson expanded BET to include one of the largest facilities for film and video production, creating jobs for hundreds of African Americans and others who otherwise might not be employed in television or a related industry.

Johnson continued to expand his reach. In 1996 the cable network launched the first black-controlled cable movie premium channel. And in 1998, Johnson created two more BET companies to produce and market films, documentaries, and television programs with African American themes.

In 1999, Viacom, Inc. purchased BET for $2.3 billion in stock. Viacom also owns MTV, VH-1, CBS, Nickelodeon, ShowTime, and Country Music Television. Many of BET's employees moved to New York after this acquisition. Johnson is the second largest individual shareholder of Viacom stock, behind Sumner Redstone, Chairman and CEO of the company.

Today, BET is in 62.4 million homes and is in over 90 percent of all black cable households. It has financed movies, published books, and operates a jazz music channel. BET continues to expand its corporate reach and is now involved in retail clothing, restaurants, hotels, casinos, financial services, and computer content development.

In 2003, Johnson set his sights on a new business venture. He is now the owner of an NBA team, the Charlotte Bobcats—bringing back a professional basketball team to Charlotte, North Carolina, after the Charlotte Hornets moved to New Orleans.

Johnson and his wife, Sheila, have two children. Over the years they have contributed to many charities, including the United Negro College Fund, Howard University, and the Levine School of Music. They also have held many charity events to help communities around the country. In June 2002, Johnson donated $1 million to the Democratic National Committee Voting Rights Institute. He also has served as a board member of the Ad Council, Minorities in Cable, the National Cable Television Association, the Walter Kaitz Foundation, and the Board of Governors of the National Cable Academy.

Among the many recognitions Johnson has received are the NAACP's Image Award (1982); the Capitol Press Club's Pioneer Award (1984); the Business of the Year Award from the Washington, D.C., Chamber of Commerce (1985); and the Turner Broadcasting Trumpet Award (1993). He also received the 1997 *Broadcasting and Cable* magazine's Hall of Fame Award and *Cablevision* magazine's

20/20 Vision Award, which named him one of the twenty most influential people in the cable industry. Johnson has been named a distinguished alumnus of Princeton University. He also serves on the boards of U.S. Airways, General Mills, and Hilton Hotels.

OPRAH GAIL

WINFREY

(B. 1954)

Oprah Winfrey's influence reaches throughout the world through her television show, magazine, and other outlets. In June 1998, *Time* magazine named Winfrey one of the one hundred most influential people of the twentieth century. In January 2001, *Newsweek* magazine selected her as "Woman of the Century." Oprah's tenacity and confidence have made her one of the wealthiest individuals in the world. In 2003, Oprah Winfrey joined the elite list of the world's richest people when she was included in *Forbes* magazine's list of billionaires. The little girl who played in bare feet on the dirt roads of Kosciusko, Mississippi, grew up to become the first African American woman billionaire.

Oprah was born on January 29, 1954, in Kosciusko to Vernon Winfrey and Vernita Lee. When Oprah was a small child, her parents, who were never married, broke up. She and her mother lived with her grandmother Hattie Mae Lee on a small farm. There was no indoor plumbing, only an outhouse, and her grandmother boiled water to wash clothes. Oprah spent the first six years of her life with her maternal grandparents. She called her grandmother Momma, but feared her grandfather.

Winfrey's intellectual abilities were evident at an early age. At age three, Oprah's grandmother taught her to read the Bible. Within a short while, she was reciting verses at the Faith United Mississippi Baptist Church. She had few playmates and spent much of her time reading Bible stories to animals around the farm. She was not shy. Her talent as a speaker began to develop at this early age.

Life was difficult for young Oprah, emotionally and socially. She got away from these problems by reading and dreaming about her future. Her grandmother encouraged her to have big dreams and to believe she could be anything she wanted.

When Oprah was four, her mother left Kosciusko and moved to Milwaukee, where she found employment as a house cleaner. When she was six, Oprah went to live with her mother. Oprah moved a lot as a young child. After living with her mother for two years, at age eight she went to live with her father in Nashville, Tennessee, because her mother could not adequately care for her and her half-sister, Patricia Lloyd. This was Oprah's third home in just a few years. She welcomed the stability of her father's home, where she was required to work hard and be well disciplined in her behavior and schoolwork.

Her father served as a deacon at Progressive Baptist Church in Nashville. He and his daughter attended church every Sunday. Oprah was an outstanding elementary school student at Wharton Elementary School in Nashville. She excelled in mathematics, reading, and science, and she outpaced her peers on achievement tests. Oprah was known to entertain other students on the playground with discussions about the sermon at church on Sunday.

At age fifteen, Oprah began to keep a journal in which she wrote about her feelings. She maintained excellent grades in school, and was sure to receive an academic scholarship when she finished high school. At age seventeen, Oprah was selected Miss Black Tennessee and competed in the Miss Black America pageant in 1971. She was also Miss Fire Prevention in Nashville that year. While a gifted high school student, Oprah began working as an announcer at station WVOL. Her radio program was highly rated in the Nashville area. Oprah was encouraged by her employer to consider a career in television.

Oprah's father encouraged his daughter to consider Tennessee State University (TSU), which was located near her father's home, so he could monitor her studies. Oprah excelled at TSU and developed her interest in radio and television. She always had a talent for communication, because she was quite articulate and loved to talk.

At age nineteen, Oprah followed the advice of her employer and became the youngest and first African American reporter for WTVF-TV in Nashville. This assignment led to a job in Baltimore where she worked for WJZ-TV, the ABC affiliate, from 1976 to 1983. Oprah received more attention in Baltimore than in Nashville because it was a bigger city with a bigger audience. Coanchoring the six o'clock news, she advanced quickly in her new assignment, moving from news anchor to cohost of a popular show called *People Are Talking*.

In 1984, Oprah made another important move, this time to Chicago. She revived a fledgling local morning talk show called *A.M. Chicago*. Almost immediately her show became nationally syndicated, and soon it was the most popular talk show in the country. Her star continued to rise while hosting that show. Within a year, she got the chance of a lifetime in *The Oprah Winfrey Show*, now the longest-running talk show in America. The show is seen in more than 106 countries, with thirty million viewers a week in the United States alone. It has been the number-one talk show for all but one year that it's been on and has received thirty-five Emmy awards.

Oprah wanted to have control over the production of her show and knew she had the talent to do it. In 1986, she started her own production company, named Harpo, which is her name spelled backwards.

Oprah also made her debut as an actress around this time. She played the role of Sofia in the critically acclaimed movie *The Color Purple*. Oprah received an Academy Award nomination and a Golden

Globe nomination for her role in this movie. A year later, Oprah appeared in *Native Son,* based on the novel by Richard Wright. Oprah also played the role of Sethe in the movie *Beloved,* based on the novel by Toni Morrison. She has also appeared in other films, including *There Are No Children Here, The Women of Brewster Place,* and *Before Women Had Wings.*

Oprah believes that education is the answer to improving people's circumstances. She has contributed millions of dollars to institutions whose mission is to provide educational and leadership programs. Her financial contributions have changed the lives of countless children and youth.

In 1997, Oprah contributed $1 million to A Better Chance, an organization that tries to give minority students the best education possible. Since 1963, the organization has given 11,500 talented students of color the opportunity to study at some of the nation's best college preparatory schools.

In 1994, Oprah donated $1 million to Providence-St. Mel School in Chicago, an independent kindergarten-through-twelfth-grade college preparatory program. That same year, Oprah contributed $3 million to Hull House in Chicago, which was founded by Jane Addams in 1889 as a settlement house for poor families. Oprah contributed $1 million in 1994 and another $1 million in 1997 to Morehouse College in Atlanta, Georgia, to fund scholarships. In February 2004, Oprah presented Morehouse College president Dr. Walter Massey with another check for $5 million to fund scholarships at the Atlanta school. This gift brings to $12 million Winfrey's total contributions to Morehouse, making her the institution's most generous individual donor. Scholarships Winfrey has funded at Morehouse have helped about 250 students continue or complete their education. In addition, Spelman College received $1 million from Oprah in 1995 to bolster the study of environmental biology, atomic physics, laser spectroscopy, and synthetic chemistry.

In 2000, the talk show host gave $10 million to build the Oprah Winfrey Leadership Academy for Girls in Henley-on-Klip, a town just outside of Johannesburg, South Africa. Ground was broken for the school in 2002. Set to open in 2005, the school will eventually have 450 students.

Oprah has also encouraged others to give of themselves. Her show began The Angel Network, to give money Oprah had donated and money from her viewers to various charities and organizations around the country.

Oprah, a phenomenal woman, finds time to be involved in many other activities. In 1999, she began teaching a class with her partner Stedman Graham at the J. L. Kellogg Graduate School of Management at Northwestern University. She assisted in establishing the Oxygen Media Company, which includes a women's cable network. In April 2000, Oprah launched *Oprah Magazine,* a monthly publication that provides articles about self-help and personal-growth topics. This magazine, much like any other Oprah project, is one of the most successful magazines in history.

Oprah has received numerous awards and honorary degrees for her achievements. She continues to encourage others to reach their dreams while speaking around the country at colleges and universities.

She has spoken out about abuse and neglect in families as well. Her commitment to children extended to testimony before the U.S. Senate Judiciary Committee to establish a national database of convicted child abusers. On December 20, 1993, then President Bill Clinton signed into law the "Oprah Bill"—the National Child Protection Act.

Oprah is still the humble person she has always been. A lawyer who managed her business affairs once said, "She still has both feet on the ground. She just wears better shoes."

SHELTON "SPIKE" JACKSON
LEE
(B. 1957)

Shelton Jackson Lee was born in Atlanta on March 20, 1957, to Jacquelyn and Bill Lee. The nickname "Spike" was given to him when he was an infant. Lee's mother, a schoolteacher, and his father, an accomplished jazz musician, introduced him to African American history at an early age. They exposed him to art, literature, the theatre, and role models who instilled pride in his identity as an African American. His father gave him early lessons in jazz and folk music that included songs by Miles Davis and Odetta.

When Spike and his siblings were of school age, their parents gave them an option of attending the predominantly white private school where his mother taught or the local public school, which was predominantly African American. Spike decided he would attend the neighborhood school where he would be with his friends.

Throughout public school, Spike was a talented student. He developed an interest in art, music, and filmmaking at an early age. When he graduated from high school, he was convinced he would pursue a career in filmmaking. After graduation, he chose Morehouse College,

the college his father and grandfather had attended. His mother and grandmother had graduated from Spelman College across the street from the Morehouse campus. At Morehouse, Spike chose to major in mass communications, a step toward becoming a filmmaker. This major would teach Spike about film, TV, print journalism, and radio.

Spike's mother died in 1977. Her death was a great loss for the family because she was not just a mother but also a friend, a mentor, and a confidante. In an effort to cheer him up, Spike's Morehouse friends began taking him to movies. He quickly became a fan of directors such as Martin Scorsese, Bernardo Bertolucci, and Akira Kurosawa. While he was impressed with these directors, he especially fell in love with the work of director Michael Cimino. After seeing the movie *The Deer Hunter*, Spike was convinced he would spend his life making movies.

In the summer of 1977, Spike could not find a job. He bought a Super 8 camera and went around New York City, shooting whatever interested him. The result was his first film, *Last Hustle in Brooklyn*.

After finishing Morehouse, Spike decided to pursue a career in filmmaking. He enrolled in the Tisch School of Arts graduate film program at New York University. Only one of a few African American students, Spike began working hard on his film projects.

Spike made a film called *Joe's Bed-Stuy Barbershop: We Cut Heads* for his master's thesis. He received the 1983 Motion Picture Arts and Sciences Student Academy Award for this forty-five-minute film. Based on his experiences living in the Bedford-Stuyvesant area of Brooklyn, this movie was the beginning of Spike's tackling of issues that affect African Americans.

His award brought him recognition but not enough money to live on. To survive, he took a job at a movie distribution house. In the meantime, Spike sought financial support for his filmmaking from his classmates. Like many other future African American millionaires, he worked hard on projects and faced adversity. At one point he thought of giving up on filmmaking, then reconsidered. He would be failing himself if he gave up on his dream.

In 1984 Spike diligently worked on a semi-autobiographical film, *The Messenger*, about a young bicycle messenger, in anticipation of receiving financial support for its production. Failing to receive adequate funding, Spike abandoned the project. Although the film was not made, Spike learned invaluable lessons that would help him deal with adversity in the future.

In 1986, Spike had his first commercial success: *She's Gotta Have It*. Produced in just twelve days, Lee had used personal savings, loans from family members, and credit cards to raise the $175,000 to make the film. It went on to make $8.5 million, and it earned him the Prix de Jeunesse at the Cannes Film Festival in 1986.

His name was now more well known, which made getting funding easier. Island Pictures agreed to support Lee's second film, a musical called *School Daze*. Following Lee's tradition of presenting real-life problems, the film was an exposé of color discrimination within the African American community. Based on his experience at Morehouse, Lee was inspired to expose the color discrimination that African Americans make between being light or dark skinned. *School Daze*, released in 1988, was a hit, earning more than $15 million.

In 1989, Spike Lee released the film *Do the Right Thing*. It was a story about the racial tension between Italian Americans and African Americans in the Bedford-Stuyvesant section of Brooklyn. One issue the film addressed was the beating and killing of blacks by the police. The film was critically acclaimed. *Do The Right Thing* was nominated for Best Original Screenplay, Best Film, and Best Director awards from the Los Angeles Film Critics Association.

Spike Lee went on to make *Mo' Better Blues, Jungle Fever,* and *Malcolm X*. Lee's fight was not over. Lee had to fight for his right to direct *Malcolm X*. Warner Brothers had planned to use Norman Jewison as the director, but Lee could not conceive of a white man directing a film about Malcolm X. He won his battle when Jewison agreed to step down as director of the film. At the same time, Lee faced criticism from a group headed by poet and activist Amiri Baraka (formerly LeRoi Jones) that Spike was not suitable to direct a film about such a great leader as Malcolm X.

Lee's fight was not over. He had initially requested $40 million for the film, but Warner Brothers only offered $20 million. Now he had to figure out how to raise the rest. Lee gave a portion of his $3 million salary and sold foreign rights to the film for $8.5 million. While conducting research, Lee discovered that Malcolm talked a lot about self-reliance of African Americans. He took the lesson to heart and called on Bill and Camille Cosby, Oprah Winfrey, Magic Johnson, Tracy Chapman, Prince, and Janet Jackson. All of them came through and wrote six-figure checks. The support from these individuals gave Spike creative control over the film.

Malcolm X was well-received by moviegoers and critics. The film raised Malcolm X to mythic status. It informed, entertained, and educated many black youth and others about the contributions of this great man. The film also placed Spike Lee in a position to negotiate with Hollywood studios for other projects.

Lee now has numerous movies to his credit, including *Crooklyn,* a film about an African American middle-class family growing up in Brooklyn; *Clockers,* a story of two brothers, one a drug dealer and the other a straight-laced family man, who become suspects in a murder investigation in the black community; and *Get on the Bus,* a story about a busload of African American men heading from Los Angeles to Washington, D.C., for the Million Man March. In 1996, Lee released two movies, *Girl 6* and *Four Little Girls,* the story of the victims of a bombing at the Sixteenth Avenue Baptist Church in Birmingham, Alabama, which earned a nomination for an Academy Award.

Other films include *He Got Game, Bamboozled,* and *The Original Kings of Comedy.* Lee has also been the executive producer on many other films.

In addition to Lee's achievements in feature films, he has produced and directed numerous music videos for such artists as Miles Davis, Anita Baker, Public Enemy, Bruce Hornsby, Tracy Chapman, Chaka Khan, Stevie Wonder, and Branford Marsalis. His short films for Home Box Office include *Iron Mike Tyson* (1991) and *Real Sports "John Thompson" Coach* (1995).

Lee has published several books, including *Spike Lee's Gotta Have It: Inside Guerrilla Filmmaking* (1988); *Uplift the Race: The Construction of* School Daze (1989); *Do the Right Thing: A Spike Lee Joint* (1990); *Mo' Better Blues* (1991); *5 for 5* (1992); *By Any Means Necessary: The Trials and Tribulations of Making* Malcolm X (1993); and most recently he and his wife coauthored the children's book *Please Baby Please*.

Spike Lee has received numerous awards and recognition for his filmmaking. The NAACP presented him with the Hall of Fame Award in 2003. Lee has received several honorary doctorates for his contributions to film, videography, and literature from Brooklyn College, Emerson College, Pratt Institute, New York University, and Princeton University.

Lee is married to Tanya Lynette Lewis, an attorney. The two met in September of 1992 during the Congressional Black Caucus weekend. They are the proud parents of a daughter, Satchel, named for Satchel Paige, the great pitcher of the Negro Baseball League, and a son, Jackson Lee. Spike Lee works with students interested in film and directing. He has made financial contributions to Morehouse College, his alma mater.

RUSSELL
SIMMONS

(B. 1957)

Russell Simmons has played a big part in the success of rap music and hip-hop. This multimillionaire first heard rap as a twenty-year-old student at City College of New York when he listened to Kurtis Blow at the Charles Gallery on 125th Street in New York City. After hearing him rap, Simmons began to promote block parties and hip-hop music with rappers such as Grandmaster Flash, Kurtis Blow, and others.

Eventually, Simmons became the founder and CEO of Rush Communications, which ranked sixteenth in *Black Enterprise*'s April 2002 issue of the top one hundred black business owners. His charitable contributions have included donations to Hale House, Harbour House, the Fresh Air Fund, Impact Repertory Theatre, Youth Speaks New York, numerous AIDS organizations, and the Stop the Violence campaign.

Simmons was born and raised in a middle-class neighborhood in the New York City borough of Queens. As a young man, Simmons was part of a gang. He left that violence behind when he discovered

a love of rap music. At his first rap show in 1977, Simmons realized that he could promote his own shows, manage artists, and produce records. Simmons dropped out of college to become Kurtis Blow's manager. He had intended to get his degree and become a college professor, but now he had a different plan. Simmons was convinced that hip-hop would have wide appeal across geographic, racial, and class boundaries. Sylvia Robinson had helped to forge the way. She was the label management behind hip-hop's first widely recognized and successful record, the Sugar Hill Gang's *Rapper's Delight*.

In 1984, Simmons and Rick Rubin, a student at New York University, founded Def Jam Records with a $4,000 investment. The record company quickly became the most important rap label in the music industry. Their first record, L.L. Cool J's *I Need a Beat*, set the company on the road to success. The founding of Def Jam Records was turned into the movie *Krush Groove* in 1985. It was a hit across the country. Although the movie only cost $3 million to make, it returned a profit of more than $20 million.

In 1985, Russell Simmons signed a production deal with CBS Records for $600,000. He began to diversify his business and promote his artists. In the year 2000, Def Jam made more than $300 million dollars. Besides the record business, Simmons has been involved with profitable movies, including *Tougher Than Leather* (1985); *Gridlock* (1995); *The Nutty Professor* (1996); *The Addiction* (1996); and *How to Be a Player* (1997).

Today, Simmons is the head of Rush Communications, a conglomerate that includes a record label, a management company (Rush Artist Management), a clothier (Phat Farm), a movie production house (Def Pictures), television shows (*Def Comedy Jam* and *Russell Simmons'* One World Music Beat), a magazine (*One World*), and an advertising agency (Rush Media Company).

Over the past twenty years, Simmons has kept up with and created trends in rap, street art, clothes, and comedy. Simmons almost never misses an opportunity to make money and think of creative ideas to market to the public. His *Def Comedy Jam,* which appears on HBO, has introduced many prominent comedians, including Chris Tucker, Steve Harvey, Jamie Foxx, D. L. Hughley, Bill Bellamy, and Martin Lawrence.

In 2000, Simmons launched an Internet site, 360hiphop.com. It features music, news, politics, lifestyle, and culture. He also produced *Def Poetry Jam,* a showcase for poetry and the spoken word that has been credited with making poetry more popular. The show was also turned into a Broadway show in 2002, discussing such issues as love, death, food, and music.

Through the years, Simmons has shared his time and wealth, working for social, political, and philanthropic causes. Simmons and his brothers Danny and Joseph founded the Rush Philanthropic Arts Foundation. This nonprofit organization is dedicated to providing disadvantaged youth with significant exposure and access to the arts. It is also dedicated to offering exhibition opportunities to emerging artists of color.

Simmons was awarded an honorary doctorate for his philanthropy in 2002 by Columbia College in Chicago. He raised $45,000, which will be used for scholarships for Chicago public high school students who want to attend Columbia College.

EARVIN "MAGIC" JOHNSON

(B. 1959)

Most individuals think of "Magic" Johnson as the outstanding NBA player of the Los Angeles Lakers. While this is the Magic that millions of viewers saw on television, there is an even bigger side to this giant of a man. He is a caring philanthropist who reaches out to others to make their lives better.

The nickname of "Magic" was a fitting one for Earvin Johnson from the moment he stepped onto the basketball court at Lansing Everett High School, and it remained so throughout his career with the Los Angeles Lakers. He was a winner from the start in the high school, collegiate, professional, and international arenas.

Earvin Johnson was born on August 14, 1959, in Lansing, Michigan, the sixth of ten children of Earvin Sr. and Christine Johnson. His father worked extra hard to support his large family. During the day he assembled cars at the local General Motors plant, and at night, he worked odd jobs. He loved basketball and spent his leisure time with his son Earvin Jr. watching basketball on television. His mother also held a full-time job as a middle school custodian.

The Johnson children never wanted for anything. There was always plenty of food, love, and discipline in the household. As a small child, Earvin Jr., with a perpetual smile, could be found on the basketball court in his neighborhood as early as 7 A.M. He claimed that one day his father and millions of other fans would watch him playing for a major NBA team. Earvin was so obsessed with basketball that he slept and ate with one by his side. Whether it was a trip to the grocery store or walking to school, Earvin always had his basketball, constantly dribbling it.

Earvin's neighbors called him "June Bug" because he was constantly jumping and hopping around the basketball court, where he welcomed any challengers, young or old, to play a game or just shoot hoops. At age fifteen, his nickname changed to Magic when he scored thirty-six points, made eighteen rebounds, and made sixteen assists during a high school game. This was phenomenal for any player at the time, and led a sportswriter to call him "Magic on the court." Throughout his career at Everett High School, Magic played basketball, and he was selected to the Michigan All-State team. During his senior year, he led his high school to the Class A championship.

Magic was convinced that he had an opportunity to be a great professional basketball player, sought after by all of the major colleges. Nevertheless, after completing high school he made a decision to stay at home and enter Michigan State University on a basketball scholarship. During his freshman year of play, Magic helped his team, the Spartans, win the Big Ten Championship over Indiana State for the 1977–1978 school year. The Spartans played in this National Collegiate Athletic Association (NCAA) championship game. Magic was excited about this match-up, as he would be playing against Larry Bird, College Player of the Year. The Spartans won easily and Magic was named the Most Valuable Player in the NCAA final-four series. The Magic-and-Bird rivalry would continue throughout the 1980s when Magic played for the Los Angeles Lakers and Bird played for the Boston Celtics.

After two years of college, Magic entered the professional basketball draft, and in 1979 he was selected in the first round to play for the Los Angeles Lakers. Lakers owner Jack Kent Cooke signed Magic to a five-year deal worth $500,000 a year, the highest salary offered a rookie to date.

Along the way, Magic married his college sweetheart, Earleatha "Cookie" Kelly. He has said that the happiest day of his life was the day he married Cookie.

When Magic began playing for the Lakers, it was not one of the top teams. Within a year Magic had an immediate impact on the league, making the Lakers the team to beat and Magic a superstar. During his twelve-year career with the Lakers, Magic led the team to five NBA titles and twelve winning seasons. He was also a twelve-time NBA All-Star. Magic was selected the Most Valuable Player (MVP) of the 1990 and 1992 seasons as well as named the NBA MVP player in 1987, 1989, and 1990.

Magic is perhaps one of the greatest role models in the history of sports. His influence was readily apparent as youth of all colors throughout the world wore his Lakers jersey with his number, 32.

On November 7, 1991, Johnson was faced with a battle off the basketball court when he was diagnosed as having the Human Immunodeficiency Virus (HIV), which is passed from person to person through bodily fluids like blood. The disease weakens the immune system, which helps to fend off diseases and keep you healthy. Magic's greatest worry was how he was going to tell his wife. Cookie stood by him, and for more than twelve years, Magic has taken medicine to control the virus.

Even after leaving professional basketball, it was still a big part of Johnson's life. He was a member of the victorious 1992 U.S. Olympics basketball "Dream Team," which won a gold medal. In 1992, Magic also became a broadcaster for NBC Sports for two years, and he was vice president of the Los Angeles Lakers from 1994 to 1995. In 1993, he returned to the Lakers as head coach for the last sixteen games.

On January 29, 1996, Magic returned to the NBA as a player after a five-year absence, helping the Lakers win twenty-nine of their last forty games. After less than a year with the Lakers, Magic retired again and turned his attention to television. His decision was prompted by the fear of other players that they would contract HIV if Magic got hurt on the court. He signed a deal with Twentieth Century Fox TV to develop, produce, and host his own late-night talk show, *The Magic Hour*.

After his career in basketball, he began to turn his magic to other interests, which included establishing a foundation, investing in businesses, and making philanthropic contributions to inner city youth. The Magic Johnson Foundation, a nonprofit organization, directs its efforts toward the health, educational, and social needs of inner city youth. The foundation has raised more than $20 million dollars to date.

Johnson's business investment in movie theaters, restaurants, a bank, and shopping centers has an estimated value of $500 million. In 1994, he formed a partnership with the Sony Entertainment motion picture group. He also developed multiplex movie theatres, called the Magic Johnson Theatres, in Atlanta, New York City, Houston, and Cleveland. Magic was inspired to start these businesses to provide economic development and jobs in local communities and improve the quality of life in inner-city neighborhoods. His franchises, including T.G.I. Friday's, Starbucks, and Fatburger restaurants, have helped to revive several inner-city communities.

Johnson also realizes the importance of bringing technology to inner-city youth and adults to bridge the gap in accessibility. In 2002, the foundation opened the eighth Magic Johnson and Hewlett-Packard Inventor Center at Taino Towers in East Harlem, New York, offering training, skills development, and access to online services for Harlem-area youths and adults. Hewlett-Packard and Johnson have established seven centers in four other inner-city communities in Los Angeles, Washington, D.C., Atlanta, and Chicago.

Magic Johnson was elected to the Basketball Hall of Fame in 2002. The father of three children, he has made many contributions toward making life better for countless individuals. He has raised over $10 million for the United Negro College Fund, and helped raise $1.5 million to support the Muscular Dystrophy Foundation. He has also contributed to the Make a Wish Foundation, the Straight Foundation, the American Heart Association, and the National Urban League, and he is a trustee for the American Cancer Society Foundation.

While he has received many awards and honors, including being recognized on the Hollywood Walk of Fame, his greatest reward is for his humanitarian efforts.

EDMONDS

(B . 1 9 5 9)

Kenneth "Babyface" Edmonds got his first taste of show business in the sixth grade when he sat in with his brother Melvin's band at a high school dance.

Since that time this multimillionaire has written and produced hundreds of hit songs for other artists. Babyface is one of the most successful producers in the music business. He may well be the best. His genius is apparent whether strumming an acoustic guitar with Eric Clapton or rapping with Snoop Dogg.

Babyface was born Kenneth Edmonds in Indianapolis, Indiana, on April 10, 1959, one of six boys in a large musical family. His father died of lung cancer when he was thirteen. The first composition of this shy boy was a love song written for a classmate named Rhonda on whom he had a crush in the sixth grade.

He graduated from North Central High School in 1976. By that time, he was already performing with bands in clubs and lounges throughout the Midwest. Edmonds began his professional career as a teenager, performing in Bootsy Collins's backup band. Edmonds got

tagged with his nickname "Babyface" when he walked into a studio and Parliament Funkadelic bassist Bootsy Collins yelled, "What's up, Face? What's up, Babyface?" The name stuck and members of the band and his audience continued to call him by his nickname.

In the mid 1970s, Babyface was a member of a band called Tarnished Silver. He also appeared in the 1970s with a band called Manchild. Some time later, he joined the funk group The Deele, which included Antonio "L. A." Reid. The Deele released three albums during the 1980s. In 1988, Babyface cowrote their biggest hit, *Two Occasions*. After leaving the group, Edmonds began his solo career, releasing his 1987 debut album *Lovers* on Solar Records.

In 1989, Edmonds formed the highly successful Atlanta-based record label LaFace with L. A. Reid. He has written and produced songs for Madonna, Celine Dion, TLC, Mariah Carey, Aretha Franklin, Boys II Men, and more. The 1992 Boyz II Men song "End of the Road" became one of the biggest-selling singles of all time.

Edmonds was named one of *Time* magazine's 25 Most Influential People in 1997. He has received a record-breaking twelve Grammy nominations. In 1999, he received a Golden Globe nomination for Best Original Song in the film *Anna and the King*.

Edmonds has shared his wealth and time with others throughout his career. He raised over $500,000 for the Little Blue House, a transitional home for abandoned babies in Washington, D.C. As a former national spokesman for the Boarder Baby Project, a group that helps abandoned children, he has raised money and awareness for these children. He has also personally donated over $100,000 to the VH1 Save the Music Program. Performing in numerous concerts, Edmonds has raised funds for acquired immunodeficiency syndrome (AIDS) research, prevention, and treatment around the world, specifically targeting Africa. In July 2001, Edmonds and former president Bill Clinton teamed up to fight AIDS in Africa and other areas with a campaign that included two concerts and a benefit album.

In 2002, Edmonds appeared at the Andre Agassi Grand Slam for Children concert in Las Vegas. The Andre Agassi Charitable Foundation (AACF) is a nonprofit organization established in 1994 to benefit at-risk youth in southern Nevada. To date, the AACF has raised more than $18 million for its charities.

Edmonds is married to Tracey McQuarn, a Stanford University graduate who enrolled at age sixteen. They have two sons, Brandon and Dylan. He and his wife formed a film production company that produced the film *Soulfood*, which grossed more than $43 million. The film also earned five NAACP Image Awards. Edmonds built Brandon Way, a private, state-of-the-art recording studio in Hollywood a few years ago and named it after his firstborn son.

Edmonds's philanthropy has not gone unnoticed. His hometown of Indianapolis has honored him by naming a twenty-mile stretch of Interstate 65 as the Kenneth "Babyface" Edmonds Highway.

TYRA
BANKS

(B. 1973)

Tyra Banks has made her mark as a top fashion model and gained worldwide attention. Banks was the first African American woman to sign with a major cosmetics company. She is one of the richest supermodels in the world, with a personal wealth of more than $10 million.

Banks was born in Los Angeles on December 4, 1973, to Carolyn and Don Banks. Although her parents divorced when she was only six years old, she grew up in a happy environment. Her mother, who worked as a medical photographer for NASA's Jet Propulsion Lab, taught her never to let anyone tell her she could not achieve her dreams. Tyra learned early in life that the only person she could compete with was herself.

It is hard to believe that Tyra Banks was a tall, skinny, and awkward adolescent. Her older brother Devin and other kids frequently teased her at school, causing her to cry and run home to her mother for comfort. When Banks attended an all-black private elementary school, the kids often called her horrible names for being so skinny.

But by the time she enrolled in a mixed junior high school, white kids thought she was the most gorgeous girl in the school. In high school, she began to fill out her skinny frame and was regarded by all her peers as both beautiful and kind.

Tyra was an excellent student in school. She got her start in modeling in high school after a friend told her that she looked like a model. By age fifteen, she had already appeared in *Seventeen* magazine, and graced her first cover at age seventeen. Prior to finishing high school, she was turned down by four modeling agencies, but Banks did not let these rejections change her career plans.

Her break into modeling came after she completed high school, when she signed with the Elite Modeling Agency at age seventeen. A scout for a French modeling agency saw her and offered Tyra a job in the fall fashion shows in Paris. Although she had been accepted by five colleges, she moved to Paris for a year and modeled for numerous big names in fashion, including Ralph Lauren and Chanel. After her assignments, she returned to the United States with plans to go back to school. She never did because her career in modeling took off.

Banks began an acting career with a small part in the British television movie *Inferno,* playing the role of a supermodel. She had a recurring supporting role on the television show *The Fresh Prince of Bel Air*. Her first serious movie role was in John Singleton's *Higher Learning,* playing the girlfriend of Omar Epps. Her performance was well received and more movie offers followed.

But Banks chose to concentrate on her modeling career instead of acting. She has appeared on the cover of several magazines, and she was the first African American model to appear on the cover of the *Sports Illustrated* swimsuit edition. Other firsts for Banks include being the first African American woman to be featured on the covers of *GQ* magazine and the *Victoria's Secret* catalog.

As a supermodel, Banks stays in shape by playing lots of sports, especially basketball, tennis, and volleyball. She runs three miles, five times a week. Although she's not on a strict diet and loves to eat barbecued ribs, fried chicken wings, fast food, and ice cream, her active exercise programs keep her in shape. Banks believes that food should be something to be enjoyed.

Banks is the author of *Tyra's Beauty Inside and Out*. In this book she offers helpful hints in developing healthy habits and provides suggestions for enhancing young women's appearances.

Banks feels blessed to have such a lucrative career and believes in sharing the wealth. In 1994, Banks started the Tyra Banks scholarship. Banks loves children, animals, and the environment. She speaks at schools and encourages kids to get a good education and become good citizens. She also promotes a line of greeting cards for the Children and Families organization, which is dedicated to helping abused and neglected children. Her love for the environment is demonstrated in her trip to the Costa Rican rainforest, during which she highlighted the plight of the endangered ecosystem in that country.

Tyra Banks founded the Banks Foundation to encourage and empower young women. They attend a weeklong summer camp where they are introduced to ways to boost their self-esteem, discussing issues like beauty and body image, relationships, and girls' mistrust of each other.

Banks has appeared in numerous films, including *Larceny, Coyote Ugly, Love and Basketball, Felicity, The Apartment Complex,* and *Higher Learning*. She is currently the executive producer of UPN's *Supermodel*. This reality television program has been so successful that it has been picked up for a second season.

ELDRICK "TIGER"
WOODS

(B. 1975)

T iger" Woods earned an estimated $447 million in 2002 and may become the world's first billion-dollar athlete. He and his father dreamed big and Tiger pushed himself toward his goal. It seems that from infancy he was destined to become a great golf player.

Tiger Woods was born on December 30, 1975, in Orange County, California, the year that Lee Elder became the first African American to play in the Masters Tournament. Tiger's father, Earl Woods, and his mother, Kultida Punsawad, met while Woods was stationed in Thailand. She is Chinese, Thai, and Caucasian. Earl Woods was a retired Green Beret and a lieutenant colonel in the Army who had served two tours of duty in Vietnam. He gave his son the nickname Tiger after a Vietnamese soldier he had befriended in Vietnam.

Woods was blessed with a father who both mentored and coached him. An avid golfer, Earl knew that black children did not get the opportunities to play golf that white children did because they were not allowed at many golf clubs. He was determined to change this situation.

Tiger Woods's road to becoming a golfer began when he was still in a high chair. While many parents were giving their children pacifiers and rattles to keep them quiet, his father chose to give him a putter. He would also hit golf balls in the garage for hours while Tiger watched.

Earl Woods knew the importance of sports in building self-esteem and confidence. He was the first African American baseball player in the Big Seven Conference (now the Big Eight) in the 1950s. Woods also knew about segregation. He had to eat at restaurants away from his teammates because of his race.

By age three, Tiger was already proficient at golf, shooting in the high 40s for nine holes. In 1978, a three-year-old Tiger appeared on *The Mike Douglas Show* in a putting contest with comedian Bob Hope. His father, the biggest influence in his life, used to sit by Tiger's bed at night and give him confidence, always telling him how good he was going to be at life and at golf. The Woodses instilled in him a sense that he could succeed at anything he tried.

Practicing on the Navy Course in Cypress, California, Tiger soon became a whiz at the game of golf. At age six, Tiger made his first birdie on a ninety-one-yard par three. Two years later, he was ready to compete. His father got him ready for his first tournament by playing subliminal tapes to improve his mental game. He trained Tiger to ignore distractions while he was trying to swing. At age eight, Tiger won the first of six Optimist International Junior World titles.

Tiger is the only player in the United States Golf Association (USGA) to have won both the Junior Amateur and Amateur titles. In 1992, at age sixteen, he played in his first professional tournament, the Nissan Los Angeles Open. He triumphed by winning the U.S. Junior Amateur Championships in 1991, 1992, and 1993, and the U.S. Amateur title in 1994, 1995, and 1996.

While Tiger spent many hours playing golf, his parents insisted that he work hard in school, and he was an excellent student. Tiger's parents taught him core values and goals that would guide him throughout life. They taught him discipline and pride in being of African American and Asian descent. Tiger received important lessons from both of his parents on how to disregard racism and achieve.

Participating in various tournaments required many sacrifices. The Woods family didn't take vacations because money was needed to transport Tiger to and from the tournaments. His mother for years would get up early in the morning and drive him to golf events throughout California. She also was the scorekeeper: Tiger was undefeated in thirty Southern California junior golf events.

After finishing Western High School, Tiger enrolled at Stanford University, one of the most highly regarded colleges in the country, on a golf scholarship. He pursued a major in economics and continued playing golf on the golf team. Tiger won the NCAA title while he was there. He decided to leave Stanford after two years and turned professional in 1996. That year he played in eight official PGA Tour events, and won two of them. Shortly after leaving Stanford, Tiger signed a $40 million promotional deal with Nike and a $20 million deal with Titleist golfing equipment.

In 1997, at the age of twenty-one, Tiger became the youngest player in history to win the Masters and the first person of African or Asian descent to win a major golf championship. His phenomenal success placed him at number one on the Official World Golf Ranking on June 15, 1997. That year he was selected as the Associated Press Male Athlete of the Year and ESPN Male Athlete of the Year.

Even when Tiger was at the top of his game, he faced some discrimination. Traditionally, the winner of the Masters selects the menu for the victory dinner. After Tiger won the Masters, fellow golfer Fuzzy Zoeller commented that Tiger should not serve fried chicken or collard greens at the celebration (he later apologized).

As one of golf's most accomplished players, Tiger seemed to break all golf records. By 1999, his success reached heights that people in the golf world could not imagine. That year, he won eight times on the PGA Tours, including the PGA Championship, and earned $6,616,585, more than most professional golfers make in a lifetime.

From 1997 through 2000, Tiger also had international victories. He won the 1997 Asian Honda Classic. In 1998, he won the Johnnie Walker Classic. He went on to win the 1999 Deutsche Bank Open and the 2000 Johnnie Walker Classic, as well as the 2000 U.S. Open in Pebble Beach, California. Tiger was the number-one ranked player in the world, and he won all four major titles that year: the PGA Championship, the Masters, the U.S. Open, and the British Open.

On March 23, 2003, Tiger went down in golf record books for his win at the Bay Hill Invitational Golf tournament. He was the first player in 73 years to win the same tournament four years in a row.

By age twenty-four, Tiger had become one of the most recognized individuals in the world. By some accounts, ratings of televised golf games rise by 40 percent when Tiger plays a tournament and by almost 100 percent when he is among the leaders. Tiger has single-handedly sparked a boom in the world of golf, packing tournaments with fans and courses with newly inspired golfers. He became the most sought after athlete to do commercial endorsements, including a deal with Buick valued at an estimated $30 million; a $100 million, five-year pact with Nike, the richest sports endorsement contract ever; and a $40 million contract to be a spokesman for American Express.

Tiger's parents taught him early on in life the importance of returning some of his good fortune to the community. Through his generous philanthropy, he wants to change the face of golf by introducing more inner-city youth and minorities to the sport. In 1996, he established the Tiger Woods Foundation to provide inner-city youth with scholarships and access to golf courses. The mission of the Tiger Woods Foundation is to empower young people to reach their potential by developing and supporting community-based programs that promote the education, health, and welfare of all of America's children.

The Tiger Woods Foundation supports six different golf clinics for youths in Orlando, Chicago, New York City, Dallas, Miami, and Memphis. In addition to teaching golf, the clinics also help youngsters to become better people. Woods has touched the lives of thousands of youth each year at clinics for his Tiger Woods Foundation.

In March 2003, the foundation announced the establishment of the Tiger Woods Learning Center. The landmark project for underserved youth will include a 35,000-square-foot education center, which will house a computer lab, auditorium, and state-of-the-art media resource center. Tiger Woods kicked off the fundraising for this $25 million center by pledging $5 million.

The Tiger Woods Learning Center will offer youth a hands-on approach to academics and other personal-enrichment experiences to help them build self-esteem and improve academic achievement. Golf will be an activity at the center, with a twenty-three-acre golf teaching facility, consisting of a thirteen-acre practice area and putting course and a ten-acre par-three course.

Tiger lives in Orlando, Florida in Isleworth, a development on the west side of Orlando. He has two half brothers and a half sister from his father's first marriage. He is engaged to Elin Nordegren, a Swedish model. He is working on two golf books for Warner Books for which he has a contract of $2.2 million.

BIBLIOGRAPHY

Banks, Tyra. *Tyra's Beauty Inside and Out*. New York: HarperCollins, 1998.

Bell, Janice Cheatham. *Famous Black Quotations*. New York: Warner Books, 1995.

Christian, Charles M., and Sari Bennett. *The African American Experience*. New York: Houghton Mifflin, 1995.

Cowan, Tom, and Jack Maguire. *Timelines of African American History*. New York: Berkley Publishing Group, 1994.

Demaratus, DeEtta. *The Force of a Feather*. Salt Lake City: University of Utah Press, 2002.

Dingle, Derek T. *Black Enterprise Titans of the B.E. 100s*. New York: John Wiley & Sons, 1999.

Ebony Editors. *Ebony Pictorial History of Black America*. Chicago: Johnson Publishing Company, 1971.

Gaston, A. G. *Green Power: The Successful Way of A. G. Gaston*. Montgomery, Ala.: Troy State University Press, 1971.

Graves, Earl G. *How to Succeed in Business without Being White*. New York: Harper Business, 1997.

Haskins, Jim. *African American Entrepreneurs*. New York: John Wiley & Sons, 1998.

Hinds, Patricia. *Fifty of the Most Inspiring African Americans*. New York: Essence Books, 2001.

Ingham, John N., and Lynne B. Feldman. *African American Business Leaders*. Westport, Conn.: Greenwood Publishing, 1994.

Johnson, Earvin "Magic." *Earvin "Magic" Johnson: My Life*. New York: Crest Publishers, 1993.

Johnson, John H., Lerone Bennett, and Quinn Currie. *Succeeding against All Odds*. Amistad Press, 1993.

Jones, Quincy. *Q: The Autobiography of Quincy Jones*. New York: Broadway Books, 2002.

Lee, Spike. *Best Seat in the House*. New York: Crown Publishers, 1997.

Lewis, Reginald, and Blair S. Walker. *Why Should White Guys Have All the Fun: How Reginald Lewis Created a Billion Dollar Business Empire*. New York: John Wiley & Sons, 1994.

Nivens, Beatryce. *Success Strategies for African Americans*. New York: Plume, 1998.

Phelts, Marsha Dean. *An American Beach for African Americans*. Gainesville: University Press of Florida, 1997.

Pinkney, Andrea Davis. *Let It Shine: Stories of Black Women Freedom Fighters*. New York: Harcourt Children's Books, 2000.

Reid, Mark A. *Spike Lee's* Do the Right Thing. Cambridge: Cambridge University Press, 1997.

Ryner, Russ. *American Beach: A Saga of Race, Wealth, and Memory*. New York: HarperCollins, 1998.

Simmons, Russell. *Life and Def: Sex, Money, and God*. New York: Crown Publishers, 2001.

Smith, Jessie Carney. *Black Heroes*. Detroit: Visible Ink Press, 2001.

———. *Notable Black American Women*. Detroit: Gale Research, Inc., 1992.

Thurman, Sue Bailey. *Pioneers of Negro Origin in California*. San Francisco: Acme Publishing Company, 1952.

Vibe Editors. *Hip Hop Divas*. New York: Three Rivers Press, 2001.

Walker, Juliet E. K. *The History of Black Business in America*. New York: Macmillan Library Reference, 1998.

Woods, Earl. *Training a Tiger: A Father's Guide to Raising a Winner in Both Golf and Life*. New York: HarperCollins, 1997.

Woods, Tiger. *How I Play Golf*. New York: Warner Books, 2001.

PICTURE CREDITS

Page 8: courtesy of the California State Library; page 10: courtesy State Historical Society of Colorado; page 15: courtesy of the California State Library; page 20: courtesy of Photographs and Prints Div., Schomburg Center for Research in Black Culture, The New York Public Library/Astor, Lenox and Tilden Foundations; page 23: From Bettye Saar and Sheila Levrant de Bretteville, Biddy Mason's Place: A Passage of Time. Photographed by Ruth Wallach, USC; page 26: courtesy of The Library Company of Philadelphia; page 28: courtesy of Photographs and Prints Div., Schomburg Center for Research in Black Culture, The New York Public Library/Astor, Lenox and Tilden Foundations; page 32: courtesy of Dr. Johnetta Cole; page 35: courtesy of the Herndon Home; page 40: courtesy of Photographs and Prints Div., Schomburg Center for Research in Black Culture, The New York Public Library/Astor, Lenox and Tilden Foundations; page 44: "Annie Malone: Business Woman," 1963, Oil on canvas by William Sylvester Carter (1909–1996). Part of the Illinois Emancipation Centennial Series, courtesy of the DuSable Museum of African American History, Chicago, Illinois. Photograph by Powell Photography, Inc.; page 49: courtesy of Photographs and Prints Div., Schomburg Center for Research in Black Culture, The New York Public Library/Astor, Lenox and Tilden Foundations; page 55: courtesy of the Birmingham Civil Rights Institute; page 62: courtesy of Issues & Views; page 67: courtesy of The HistoryMakers; page 72: courtesy of AP Wide World Photos; page 78: courtesy of USC Law School; page 83: courtesy of Louisiana State University at Shreveport. Photo by Thurman Smith, Shreveport Louisiana; page 87: courtesy of AP Wide World Photos; page 93: courtesy of AP Wide World Photos; page 98: courtesy of Dudley Products Inc., photograph by Joan Moser; page 104: courtesy of TLC Beatrice International Food, New York; page 109: courtesy of AP Wide World Photos; page 115: courtesy of AP Wide World Photos; page 121: courtesy of AP Wide World Photos; page 127: courtesy of AP Wide World Photos; page 131: courtesy of AP Wide World Photos; page 137: courtesy of AP Wide World Photos; page 141: courtesy of AP Wide World Photos; page 145: courtesy of AP Wide World Photos.

INDEX

Lee, Jacquelyn, 120
Lee, Miriam, 81
Lee, Satchel, 125
Lee, Shelton "Spike" Jackson, 120–125
Lee, Vernita, 114, 116
legal profession, 50–51, 77, 80–81, 106
Leidesdorff, William Alexander, v, 2, 7–11
Leland University (New Orleans, Louisiana), 79
Lester, Peter, 20
Levine School of Music, 112
Lewis, Abraham Lincoln, 31–36
Lewis, Carolyn Cooper, 103
Lewis, Clinton, 103
Lewis, Julia Brown, 31
Lewis, Loida Nicolas, 106–107
Lewis, Reginald Francis, 103–107
Lewis, Robert, 31
Lewis, Tanya Lynette, 125
Lewis and Clarkson Law Firm, 106
Lincoln Golf and Country Club (Jacksonville, Florida), 34
literacy, slavery, 17
L.L. Cool J, 128
Lloyd, Patricia, 116
Los Angeles, 10, 25
Los Angeles Bar Association, 80
Louis, Joe, 34, 84
Louisiana State University (Shreveport), 3, 85
Lourdes, Leslie, 107
Lumet, Sidney, 90
lynchings, 51, 53

Madame C. J. Walker College of Hair Culture and Manufacturing Company, 41, 42
Madonna, 138
magazine industry, 29, 71, 75–76, 92, 95, 100, 119. *See also* newspaper industry
Magic Johnson Foundation, 134
Malcolm X, 94, 123–124
Malone, Aaron, 46
Malone, Annie Turnbo, 42, 43–47
Malone, John, 111
Manual Arts High School (Los Angeles), 79
maritime trade, 7, 9, 10
Marsalis, Branford, 125
Marshall, James, 11

Mason, Bridget "Biddy," 22–26
Mason, Charles, 52
Mason-Dixon line, 52
Masonic organizations, 33
Massey, Walter, 118
Mathis, Johnny, 89
McQuarn, Tracey, 139
McWilliams, Moses, 39
mentoring, 65, 67, 99, 101
Mexico, 9
Michigan State University (Lansing), 132
migration. See Great Migration
Mingus, Charles, 89
Missouri Compromise of 1820, 52
modeling industry, 140–143
Monk, Thelonious, 89
Morehouse College (Atlanta), 3, 118, 120, 122, 125
Morgan State University (Baltimore), 94
Mormon Church, 22, 24
Morris Brown College, 53
Morrison, Toni, 118
Mosley, Eunice, 99, 100, 101
Mother Bethel African Methodist Episcopal Church (Philadelphia), 26
mulatto, 17
music industry, 86–91, 126–129, 136–139. *See also* film industry; television industry
mutual aid associations, philanthropy, 2

National Association for the Advancement of Colored People (NAACP), 3, 30, 42, 52, 65, 74, 79, 80, 125, 139
National Association of Manufacturers, 65
National Cable Television Association (NCTA), 110–111
National Child Protection Act of 1993, 119
National Laboratories, 63
National Negro Insurance Association, 34
Negro Business League, 34
New Orleans, 7, 18
newspaper industry, 20, 29, 48, 50–53, 56, 64, 81. *See also* magazine industry
New York University Tisch School of Arts, 122
Niagara Movement, 74